SELF ARTICLE 360

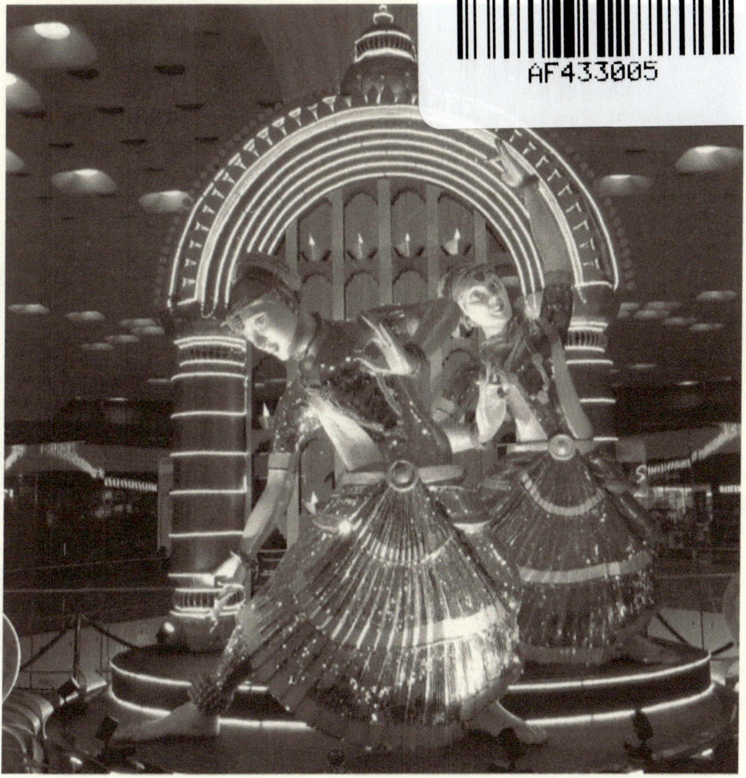

ABHIJIT ANIRUDHA VYAVAHARE

First published in 2020 by
BecomeShakespeare.com

Wordit Content Design & Editing Services Pvt Ltd,
123, Building J2, Shram Seva Premises,
Wadala Truck Terminus,
Wadala (E), Mumbai - 400037
T:+91 8080226699

ISBN: 978-93-90040-71-1

NAMASKAR ALL!

This is an initiative to portray small examples of life to make everyone's life meaningful & delightful. It should improve wealth, health, safety, nature and nation. It is applicable to all of those people who want to make their life happy and engender high respect for other human beings.

In the name of improvement, humans have created obstacles in front of humans. To regain happiness in life, this basket of articles will help in various aspects. Not only the nation, but even an individual can contribute their efforts to make life meaningful for self & others.

Humans are a very important & integral part of world. Without humans, the world has no meaning. Excess usage of technology by humans has reduced the happiness in their lives. By putting in 'extra cost' in the purchase of fast high-end vehicles, latest TV models, and mobile phones every now & then, he wants to bring happiness back in his life. Here, this book will help to search oneself at no cost and will make life successful. Happiness & success lie within oneself, and one only needs to excavate and uncover the right things at the right time.

I have seen many people who search the meaning of life & happiness in every nook and corner of life. We search for meaning of life in others. Happiness, peace, thoughts are all our own and are within us if we search within us we get it. We need to focus on our own life without being selfish. Let's try looking at every example of each article to overcome the many hurdles in our own life. My way of thought may not exactly match with everyone else's, but it will help make an excellent society, where family bonds will be much stronger & safer.

The world is facing challenges of peace, and happiness of human beings is in danger from the global warming - the damage being caused to nature. Every nation & human's contribution will help create a better future for humans. We need to get rid of increased selfishness, addiction to drugs and excess technologies, demolished education system, hidden knowledge, etc. With love & peace in hand, land is lovely, Life is meaningful & successful. Love to human & nature makes life easy, better & simple.

At no extra cost, we will try to bring all humans together and become a happy & successful family with great values.

DEDICATION

This book is written in memory of my Mother Shanta, who being an illiterate, taught me the real meaning of life, lessons of ethics, love, and the fact that the gap between poverty and richness is zero, if we just remove the ego out of it. Being a child of poverty taught me to be on track always & to live a balanced life. For every wrong thing that I did, she corrected me and taught me the right things. She never allowed anyone to bow down in front of failure. She showed confidence in the power of creativity, which carved my childhood nature beautifully. Like all Indian mothers, she hit me for all the wrong things that I did with her words, her utensils, and made my life beautiful & meaningful by putting me on the right path. I was born as a needy, which added values in my life in multiples. I remained watchful of the changing society and lifestyle and took decisions in my life to change for the better. **Healthy life is wealthy life but a wealthy life is not a healthy life!**

My mother loved me a lot, without much display. She always pushed me to be strong. She trusted my decisions and was never overconfident & over ambitious. She let me run wild & let me fly high like the birds. The freedom she gave me acted on me like a flying kite with her guiding love acting as a thread even today in her absence.

ABOUT THE AUTHOR

Education: - B.Tech Agri Engg., MMS in Marketing & Production.

24 years of professional working experience in 1 MNC & 3 OEMs. Working with the organization 'CNHI' as on date in the global manufacturing quality team. Have handled national & international goals successfully.

Health-oriented outlook, sportsmanship, and leadership used in family businesses' work culture to make family healthy, wealthy, happy, and successful in every path of life. Despite being born in an economically backward class family, aiming high made me successful, and consistent in the growth of life.

My book should make every individual's life simple, easy, successful, wealthy, healthy, & long.

Written a Marathi book - "Vicharanche Adbhut Jag" which is about how miraculous thought processes make an individual's life successful.

ACKNOWLEDGEMENTS

My Family Members - Papa, Wife, & Children who have added value to my life. My organization – CNHI – has played a very important role when it came to supporting me, my development, & enriching me with valuable experience.

PREFACE

Doctors prescribe medicines to get rid of diseases, whereas this book will teach all of us to maintain good & long health, wealth, & mind at all times. I was born in an economically backward class; our basic learnings made our lives bright & successful, when it came to health, wealth, & mind. It's because we looked for peace & happiness even in small things. We need to understand & learn, where & when to stop on the branches of life to remain connected to the tree of life.

Which super race are we trying to win? We don't know who is in front of us & who is behind us. We run an unknown race to win from unknown people. We should run a race daily for our health, and challenge ourselves to make each day brighter & better. We are all God's particle, enlightened in body from the rays of the mighty sun. So, one should make their lives effective by lightening others' lives.

India is a powerful, mysterious, and loving land, and we need to excavate our own culture, its love, and the land's real education, which has been hidden in depositories of past years, gathering dust & dirt. We have our own challenges in India, and similar challenges are being faced by the world to become a safe, healthy, peaceful place. Let us put all our efforts together to make this world beautiful and ensure a safer and better future for humans.

One can spare a few minutes from his valuable time to read small articles to gain good innovative inputs that will help make life successful, peaceful, meaningful, & beautiful.

The only thing making
you unhappy are your
own thoughts.
Change them.

CONTENTS

1.

NAMASKAR'- LORD'S WEAPON OF LOVE FOR THE WORLD!

Namaskar!

'A traditional Indian greeting or gesture of respect, made by bringing the palms together before the face or chest and bowing' is the definition that the Oxford dictionary gives us for "Namaskar". Hindi "Namaskar" comes from the Sanskrit namaskāra, namas meaning 'bowing' + kāra meaning 'action'. "Welcome" or "hello" a well wish to any human being that is performed from the heart, with joined palms, and the fingertips touching each other is called "Namaskar"!

The word "Namaskar" in the Indian culture is similar to "Good morning" in English, "Gunaydin" in Turkish,

"Buongiorno" in Italian and similar to its equivalents in other languages as well.

"Namaskar" is an exercise of POWER. When a human joins his palms in "Namaskar" real respect is observed not only with those words, but also in the position of the hands, the bowed head and in the eyes lowered with love. It is pure respect towards one another.

Apart from being a mark of respect to other humans, the "Namaskar" also helps us to recover from many health issues with its automatic acupressure effect. When respect reflects in Namaskar position, stress is reduced automatically, ego is destroyed, BP remains constant within limit, and the mind becomes free from impure thoughts.

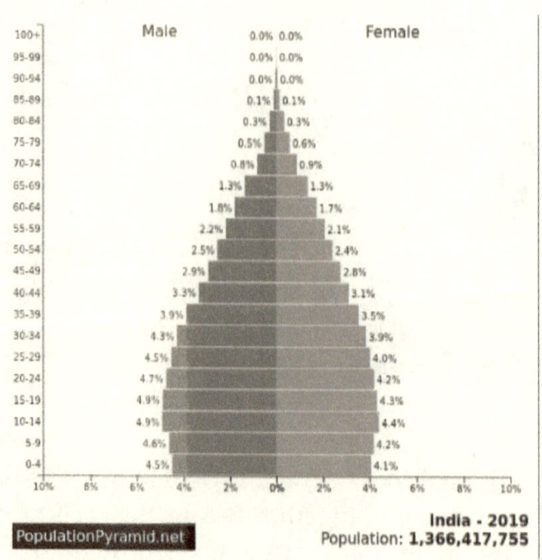

Average Life Expectancy in India 2019.

It has been pointed out in some studies that when one takes out time to pray, he or she is essentially surrendering all their fears and stress onto God making them a happier person. This state of hope and happiness can be attributed to the fact that while praying, our palms are joined in "Namaskar", and we are sending out good vibrations into the universe, positive vibes which will come back to us, making us live a longer and happier life.

Namaskar is medicine for the mind; it creates acupressure in the palms and is like a self-palm massage! Namaskar works like a strong medicine, which makes life healthy and long. In this Namaskar, we only join our own hands & don't shake them with others', thus, avoiding direct contact with unknown personalities and keeping us from contracting contagious diseases from others.

Namaskar is the enlightening of a soul to its purest path. Anyone can have a life with "No Enemies" i.e. all the world becomes united, a friend. As a result of this unity and good relationship, we experience growth and good exchange of skills with ease. The "Namaskar" is a free of cost culture, "you won't pay a penny, and still the power of the entire world will respect you."

"Namaskar" is a form of respectful love. It's a simple, powerful, effective love weapon of the world.

It helps humanity & nature to flourish, & this nature which is constructive for our minds, souls, & bodies always remains part of a human's nature. Many powerful saints like Buddha, Guru Gobind Singh ji, Sant Dnyaneshwar, Swami Vivekanand, and Mahatma Gandhi have used this tool of respect. You will see that though humans & saints may leave this world, but their gift of 'Namaskar', its roots and the routes to it are available to all humans of this world in different pronunciations or actions. Namaskar makes everyone work together without any differences in sex, age, colour, language, lifestyle etc. It teaches us the way of speaking in a good & respectful manner and to behave ethically with clean & pure thoughts.

Known & Unknown hands work together with this power on a miraculous journey. Namaskar is the mind's thought, a language's word, a hand's action, a Weapon of

Weapons, Nature's human, and the Answer to all Questions!!!

Namaskar is the way to Success! It adds to one's direct & indirect values benefits of which are not mapped on our planned path to success. It acts like a Nuclear reaction - very fast and silent. Namaskar is the focused long breath of every success. The rich history of Hindus & Inventions in science used effectively by ancient Bharat (Old Hindustan) are in practice even today. Namaskar is power, patience, and respect towards all known & unknown human values. So Namaskar is the mother of respect for love, conversion to success, peace of life. Professional organizations, tourism, & hotel industries are working with "Namaskar", respecting all human beings of creating culture of success, happiness, growth in business.

Namaskar gives strength in life & business too. It is the Light of Soul!

Our body is self-charged with many electrons. Like how the mind has 2 types of thoughts - good & bad, similarly the body is charged with Positive charge which is in the right side of the body & negative charge on the left side of the body. For a bulb to glow, it needs both positive & negative. Similarly, the body glows with strong positive aura when you do Namaskar. Namaskar has only merits no demerits. So those who practice it regularly, for them, Namaskar can lead them to live in the world with simplicity & peace.

Namaskar removes every ounce of fear from the body. Shyness doesn't touch the mind with the transparent communication of "Namaskar". When no currency or kingdom was in existence, people were living a happy life with Namaskar. Namaskar is done only by humans; no animal does it with both palms touching, which gives substantially extraordinary results to Humans in return. Namaskar makes a prayer from one soul to another a direct relationship and it may work its greatness within oneself remotely & unknowingly. Complexity becomes simple & easy with Namaskar. Soft words of peace, love, are spoken without any hidden agenda. "Namaskar" is a special weapon, which is more effective & powerful than all the latest weapons available in the world. This weapon was effectively used by Gautam Buddha, Bhagwan Mahavir, Sant Dnyaneshwar, Sant Tukaram, Sant Ramdas, Gurunanak ji, Akkalkot Swami Maharaj, Shirdi Sai Baba, Swami Vivekanand and many others. It has spread humanity worldwide.

Namaskar is the soul of Indian culture. Past rulers have gone, but humanity of every human being is increasing day by day. It shows that any weapon, either in the past or even today is ineffective in front of Namaskar! Mahatma Gandhi ji has spread humanity via Namaskar in entire world! Namaskar is for the benefit of everyone. Namaskar is the Invisible, effective weapon stronger than all of the weapons of the world. Namaskar is an effective tool of communication & works like an atomic power reactor with its vibrations continuing forever. "Namaskar!" can be used by anyone, anytime, anywhere! Do it & feel the difference in self-improvement, self-control, communication, and health management. "Namaskar" kills anger as anger kills human beings! So, think about what you need - anger or peace?

Namaskar is the beginning of Strength! Namaskar has proved its power, where the powers of money, weapons, authority have failed. Great warrior, King Shivaji, used this same weapon to increase effectiveness & respect amongst his soldiers and for the betterment of the common public. He was a kind and well-known warrior and had effective communication, management, & administration skills. He was highly respected in the society.

A namaskaram is a short series of hand and leg movements performed before and after dancing Bharatnatyam. It is believed that this is a way to take blessings from Mother Earth in order to dance better and also to apologize to her for having stamped on her while dancing.

Surya Namaskar (Sanskrit: सूर्यनमस्कार IAST: Sūrya Namaskār), Salute to the Sun or Sun Salutation, is a practice in yoga as an exercise incorporating a sequence of twelve gracefully linked asanas. The set of 12 asanas is dedicated to the Hindu God Surya. Here we see that 'Namaskar' is done to Earth (Bharatnatyam for the Earth to support us), to Sun for achieving a healthy body with exercise, to humans for improving relationships, and with any living or non-living things. It is creating wealth in terms of better body & mind health, which is the real prosperity of any human kind. Respecting nature & human is thorough symbol of 'Namaskar'.

Like the many buttons in a remote control, many controls are present in our palm. The many nerve endings in our palms make them very sensitive. A crying baby does not speak any words but a paediatrician checks the palms of the baby for pain & treats accordingly. Acupressure on palms confirms the position of the pain. The continuous pressing on pin points gives relief from pain & provides quick healing without any side effect or extra time.

According to Sadguru Jaggi Vasudev ji, 'Namaskar' is the process in which hands are put together in alignment at the level of the heart. Simplest form of Yoga is to put hands in Namaskar! The physical world is a union of polarities of masculine & feminine, ida & pida nadi, individuals & universes, right & left brain, positivity & negativity of mind & body, shiva & shakti, etc. It brings to you a certain harmony, unites you with that internal energy, likes & dislikes are leveled out & there is oneness with who you are. If we perform this namaskar for few minutes every day we will begin to harmonize; look upon someone or something that means a lot to you; it could be the sun, moon, planets, trees, clouds, mother, father, wife, husband, child or any picture that matters to you,look at that someone or something with emotions that can generate a loving attitude and attention in your namaskar, your life will be transformed. Humans are aware of their own nature of love, and blissful experiences; we can understand ourselves. Namaskar yourself into peace, love, union. Let's put our hands together & unite the world. We may unfold the world with folded hands- Namaskar!!!

Gautama Buddha
Anna Hazare
Narendra Modi

2.

LOSE TO WIN

I wanted to swim but always feared dying, so I would keep my legs on the ground inside the water. I would hear my mother's voice shouting at me, "Lift your legs from the ground & then swim." Once I was thrown in deep waters, and I swam to a great extent to save myself; that was my first swimming lesson, an experience I embarked on with fear but completed with self-confidence. Now, with 3-4 meters of swimming, I feel my happiness has reached to the extent of swimming in Olympic championships. My mother taught me, to 'leave the ground', to swim in life as well if I wish to touch the sky just don't forget the land & land safely.

Leaving is losing something - comfort zone, money,

land, etc. - to gain something - winning spirit, knowledge, money, love, etc. Strength comes from losing ourselves, to win something for ourselves. There are many, who haven't "won" in their own eyes. Definitions of losing & winning change day by day, but with a strong aim and will power, it is possible to achieve one's destination and goals. Like they say, "Every drop makes an ocean", similarly, every successful man is a Loser first! If we don't lose the battle at home on a daily basis, we won't become a winner.

Companies & entrepreneurs don't always run their businesses successfully by their own, rather they try to make smart decisions, hire people with smart skills, sign joint ventures, and mergers to make their businesses profitable.

When we lose our battles at home in front of our spouses, or children i.e. when we invest in them a lot without knowing "what will be the outcome or the ROI", it mainly works. We lose today for the long term win tomorrow. Losing adds experience to every step. If we win on the first day itself, it may keep us away from real experience & the harsh facts of life.

Scientists & innovators always find success despite their many failures; they win with a "never give up" attitude. Even in families, both the spouses stay together and live a long, happy life with this lose to win i.e. the adjustment policy. Papa's strictness & mother's love kind of policy works well to groom a child.

Everyone has a different capacity that defines "losing something." One may lose 1$ or 10$, depending on their definition of losing capacity. As an Indian, when we visit foreign countries for the first time & need to pay 1$ or 1 Euro for personal call, it is noted as something which was never budgeted for. That amount is your lost amount, which you may lose every day, every month, or every quarter to go about your own business. One day you will win, but until that day one must be habituated to losing. Any business' return becomes another business' grab in scrap value. We must increase our holding time for extracting the same. We should try and understand the changes a business needs at the right time.

Life is a race! And everyone knows it. But no one is ready to lose the race. Everyone must patiently look out for their turn & when it finally comes, should take a long breath and win. It is a fact that one cannot be a winner all day every day. It is a cycle. We should try to retain life's gained wisdom for longer periods.

Investing is losing first to win later. If we are not ready to lose, then how will we become winners, is something we must think of. "I don't have time for you", this phrase starts from home and goes beyond home as well. If we invest i.e. lose time to give to our family, then we will get good returns, same with office, every person, etc. Even in farming, when we sow the seeds in the soil, we get the natural returns of it.

If we hold gold coins in our hands & see diamonds lying in front of us, we won't be able to get the diamonds unless we are willing to let go of the gold. There is an invisible parting line the mind between Losing & Winning. One cannot be a winner everywhere. i.e. being a winner or the best in at something must be appreciated by one because even though he may not know 99.9999% of this world's knowledge, he very well knows the skills that he mastered!

Instead of running behind winning every day, one should look within, to find happiness, as humans have everything that could make his life happy. We have read about many leaders who were winners in the eyes of ordinary people like King Ashoka, King Akbar, but they themselves lost many things in life including real happiness. **We live a life of 100 years for a single successful day,** which no one other than us will remember.

Those whom we race against are competitors created by us. We should try to win our own race without creating any competition, like Baba Amte, Guru Gobind Singh ji, King Shivaji, Sant Dnyaneshwar, Sant Tukaram, Bhagwan

Mahavir, Gautam Buddha, Swami Vivekanand. They were extraordinary men, men we cannot compete with even today because they worked their entire lives for humans! They gave up, "lost" their normal lives but are winners today, examples of great human beings. We all must think why we aren't more like these people, it is because we fear to Lose, and we want to live a materialistic successful "winning" life!

3.

COMPLAINT BOX 2 HAPPY BOX

Sadhanatai Amate a great woman & a strong pillar of the leprosy recovery foundation is well known to the world. Her memorable & valuable words, thoughts, and actions in life all said one thing, **"Life is not a complaint box!"**

Every day we might find ourselves complaining based on the prevailing circumstances - water is cold today, electricity is gone again, bus is late again today, all politicians are corrupt like this, monsoon is a nuisance, complaints about wife, family & even about our own bodies. Our bigmouth & fickle mind results in us becoming a 'lifetime Complaint box' creating excuses for ourselves. We are the greatest criticizers of everything we see, hear, learn, smell, taste, and touch with all senses even the sixth sense.

We come across complaint boxes kept in malls & government office premises, etc., and have seen them accumulate a lot of dust but hardly any complaints. This has 2 meanings, either no one has any complaint, or all complaints are getting resolved on a daily basis. There is a complaint register available with every bus conductor of government buses, but they hardly give it to anyone to write on as they feel it will jeopardize their job. We stop people from complaining sometimes, which ultimately stops our improvement too & people go around the world seeking its solution. Let's not forget, "if we don't do it, someone else will." So, accept a complaint as constructive criticism and look at it as an opportunity to improve, try resolving it and work on it positively then watch the results of your actions. Results will be a wonderful, successful wrapping of your positive actions.

Many a times, customers don't speak up about what they want exactly but have a wish list, expecting a miracle to happen like with Alladin's Chirag. Mothers also don't feed their babies unless the baby is crying. So, customer demands need to be understood clearly to figure out what they need exactly.

Complaining in a constructive manner is helpful for self-improvement and is better than complaining about others, or arguing pointlessly due to over expectations and ambitions. No one likes to complain unnecessarily, so a complaint can be taken positively and be worked upon to improve oneself as the complainant may feel that there is scope of improvement if he or she complains and suggests a resolution.

Proactive market study & an efficient customer support leads to a reduction in incoming complaints thus, making a business successful as it creates time to focus on sales, market, improvement areas, and scope for innovations.

Quick complaint resolution also helps in personal life. We complain about keeping shoes & chappals in the shoe rack or clothes neatly ironed in the cupboard. Every Monday, we may find family members looking for uniforms, socks, hankies, shoes etc. It takes away our important time & makes us unnecessarily angry. Similarly, we keep on thinking without proper action & go on accumulating complaint data which keeps us from success.

"Prevention is better than Cure!" But still, many including individuals and the biggest governments allow gaps in processes or communication leading to complaints. Knowingly or unknowingly complaints get are usually a result of improper planning. In this fast life of "Breaking news", we watch this news to "Complain" about whatever is "breaking" at the speed of light – fire here, attack there, scam here, and a murder there. We need to make enormous efforts to reduce the necessity of such complaints, which is possible only if people are more aware of themselves and their surroundings, aided by a smoothly functioning government machinery. Media always helps to identify & expose the concerns of common life. Where, when, why, who, how & more such questions need to be resolved with the help of various resources working behind it. We need to collect answers from every citizen to make this world work right and also for living a long, happy life. We work on short term gain basis which result in the opening of a concern box. Some citizens & politicians would use this short term formula in the past to get materialistic or monetary benefits and even today we see some of them saying, "Let people come to me, they should know the importance of my chair & the position I hold." Now, slowly the days are changing & sufferers have started to get answers to their complaints and queries without waiting in long queues for days on end.

Those who manage to live their life with minimal or no complaints are examples of silent success stories. They keep rolling in life cross all hurdles quietly in pin drop silence. It is the beauty & power of a strong identity. Ants too, pose a similar example. The ability to talk has given humans a chance to improve his life by speaking his mind. Problems arise when humans try to "improve" for selfish reasons, thus, disturbing the lives of others and the nature.

As a kind & loving human being who is a part of nature, one should make plans, no matter how small, for the development of earth, protection of nature, & for self-growth. Keep the complaint box empty & open up the "**Happy Box**" which should be filled with lots of "**Thank you & compliments**". Convert those complaints to Happy moments every second. The problem and solution both starts with "I" & ends with "I". This one single letter depicts the direction of life – when we complaint it is horizontal, having no upward movement but when we are choosing happy moments by seeking improvement solutions we go onwards and upwards.

So **"I am the complaint box & I am the Solution Box too!"**

All humans have a Happy Box! One only needs to open it.

4.

SLOW IS BIG!

Once while returning home, a stranger, who started walking in the morning had covered almost 30 Km on foot by evening. He kept thinking and trying to understand, how Buddhism, Jainism, Varkari Sampradaya have spread love & humanity all over the world just by walking without making use of any planes. It is evident who has a better footprint over the world, the one who walks for peace, love, & knowledge, or the one who tries to conquer the world with supersonic speed.

Management studies always use the example of ants to show the correlation between their steady, systematic, and dedicated working style & their steady population growth. Investments, businesses, industries, and any life that shows rapid growth also tends to have a big downfall with immediate catastrophic effects. Slow & consistent growth lasts long & gives happiness. Almost every human being is now lacking patience and is all about the fast mode of life – mobiles, aeroplanes, and what not. These mobiles themselves vanish into thin air rapidly; you buy a phone today and there's a new one on the market the next day.

India's growth seems stable today after centuries of looting of Indian wealth, culture, and land by other countries & even by its own citizens. Economy & GDP growth though quite slow, is still on the right track, so we see stability in our self-growth and regular lifestyle. Everyone has read about the modest lifestyle & behavior of Warren Buffet & of other rich people; they live like that because they want to retain the same wealth for a longer period & not just for the day. Whereas we aim at "One day I will be rich" & what happens is that you become 'rich for a day'. As we dream, so we become. Many talented people, skillful actors, & personalities of any field – sports, music, arts, theatre, and writing – are unseen by public due to their slow and modest growth curve. But this is what makes them firm in their positions. Vehicles also have good control when they are slow; even Michael Schumacher, the fastest racing car champion, has faced a mishap. Keep moving slow for a big win!

We have read the story of the tortoise winning the race against the rabbit – **Slow and steady wins the race!** It is a fact that tortoises live for more than 100 years; we see it ourselves when we go to zoos. That which lasts long is the winner. In our regular lives now-a-days, bogged down by mobile & internet devices, we constantly search for our 'me-time' that has been missing for long. Parents often think about what's wrong with their own & their children's life's growth. We are in the gluttonous want of everything fast - food, speed & life. 'Speed of life' has increased unwantedly. We need to focus & put brakes on this uselessly fast ride to gain control on ourselves; everyone loves a safe & long life. No one wants to 'leave the life' feeling unsuccessful, unhealthy, un-wealthy, un-safe & without peace & happiness. We all have seen cars moving fast, jumping signals and then being caught later. The "Fast speed life" mentality is a poor mentality which creates undue pressure on self & on others too. So, we will learn to live simply for a long, better, safe life, and maintain consistency in winning spirit.

Slow is really Big!

Water drops forms an ocean, pennies make a billionaire by engendering a `**passion for patience**`. Simple living is a backdated concept today & is opposed by a lot of people. We need to learn living styles adopted and embodied by Mahatma Gandhiji, Swami Vivekanand, Gautam Buddha, Baba & Prakash Amate, Bhagwan Mahavir, Sant Tukaram, & Sant Dnyaneshwar to become enriched, enlightened humans & last spiritually, forever in the minds of all humans whose lives we touched. The recent ages have given us many high profile personalities like Sudha Murthy ji, Anna Hazare who live simply.

Simple is beautiful and slow is really big!

Slow life has low enemies & more robust friendships. High speed has many enemies including our own self in between our path to success. High speed life is a threat to health, wealth, & infinite growth of individual. So, humans must try to **obey natural speed of life** for a better & long life!

5.

UNPATENTED PATENT

Many people love & live for patents. It shows their love and respect towards an innovative mind-set. We are all unaware about Patents that lie with us. We need not register them, yet they remain our own & no one can steal it from us. Our face, likes, thoughts, humanity, integrity, our quirks can never be matched with others. Everyone is a uniquely identified personality that does not match with others, even in case of twins. Growing up, people may come from similar backgrounds, and situations but their views on life may differ starkly. We keep on mapping these differences but forget to map why the difference is there in the first place. It's god's gift to everyone, to have their own image & Unique Identity since birth. Since we all are different, we progress in life in different ways, and in different areas, creating value in us and in this world. So, we must value our own uniqueness and stand proud as an outstanding performer.

Our UID should keep us from comparing ourselves with each other but we still try to copy much of the prevailing practices and trends. One should focus on one's own goals & aim to reach extraordinary levels of performance to get a sense of self-reward and achievement. It's the greatest real award when we are transparent and stand as the 'right human' in our own eyes. Every other reward stayed with us only for a tiny moment, public forgets it the next. Self-award is life-long, something which does not have bindings of age, cast, religion, country. Many successful people, unknown to the world, have achieved miracles and great success in their area of interest. So, we must focus on ourselves and make ourselves patient from within. We must dig out our values, interests, qualities and help Humans & nature, which will indirectly return as a gift to us.

Love self to Love Human & Nature!

Your love is incomparable to anyone else's. It is unique! Similarly, humanity, patience, character, ethics, respect, likes, qualities etc. are incomparable. So, we must refrain from using standard rules for acceptance in parts of life. Everyone is unique in his or her qualities, which demand respect from others. Open books & Open Secrets are always in some ways hidden as it needs real vision to come forth, read, emulate, & maintain consistency. It's better to have qualities in us rather than trying to emulate others'. So, we must focus on our own qualities, and improvement to get successful results. We must say- **I'm myself & not a copy!** Maintaining our own style of qualities facilitates a long life whereas a copied life is for a short time. Let's promote self-initiatives, ideas, talents; let's speak up, breathe deep, and shout out to the world, **"You are Uniquely Identified!"**

6.

STAR PERSONALITIES

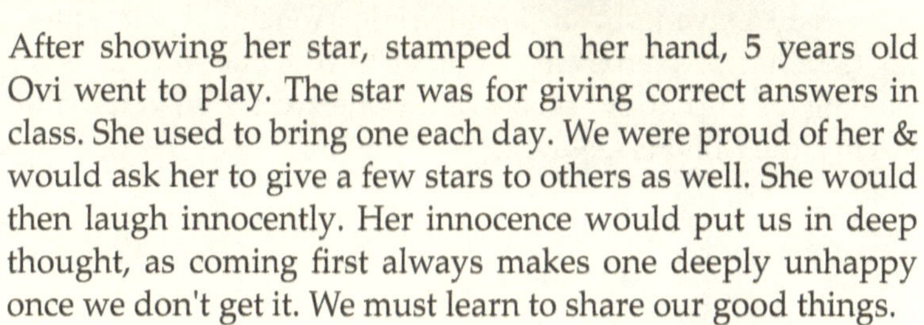

Talk to yourself at least once in a day, Otherwise you may miss a meeting with an excellent person in this world.

- Swami Vivekanand.

After showing her star, stamped on her hand, 5 years old Ovi went to play. The star was for giving correct answers in class. She used to bring one each day. We were proud of her & would ask her to give a few stars to others as well. She would then laugh innocently. Her innocence would put us in deep thought, as coming first always makes one deeply unhappy once we don't get it. We must learn to share our good things.

Star players put in extraordinary efforts in their respective games to achieve top positions and ranks. Sportsmanship is all about having a winning spirit & "never give up" attitude. They sweat and keep their efforts consistent during peaceful situations to avoid bleeding in war time.

Various competitions including Olympics have become a stage for comparison and proving superiority. We have seen that even though someone wins a gold medal in any race, competition etc. not many of us know their name. Usain Bolt, known because of his work, is the fastest man on earth & a Star personality of this world. There are many star personalities in different games & other fields who are unknown to the world. Winning consistently in our own race of life & winning just that one time for a prize to show off, has a big difference.

Spiritually powerful personalities like Guru Gobind Singh ji, Bhagwan Mahavir, Gautam Buddha, Mahatma Gandhi, Swami Vivekanand, and Sant Kabir became famous & prayed for a long period without wishing for any monetary gains like land, gold, jewels, etc. They were never in any race to become known & famous. Followers of such personalities looked up to them for peace of mind, happiness, and a healthy life.

See the difference, we "look up to" these spiritual personalities & we "follow" the Star personalities.

If we are patient and consistent in our efforts, we too will become successful and spiritually strong like the personalities we look up to.

Sant Dnyaneshwar ji said "Jo Je Wanchil, To Te Laho!" i.e. God has blessed everyone to achieve what he desires for making his life happy and peaceful. One must think differently - When the Mind is Gold, Life is Golden!

7.

ZERO MAPPING!

One night my 11-year-old young friend was trying to solve a mathematics problem - 10X10000+0X1000+1X100+10X8+7. He solved it incorrectly, but since it was late in the night, we couldn't discuss it in detail. I gave him a hint that when zero is multiplied to anything, the answer is zero. He corrected his answer & in the morning I realized what I was talking about.

In real life, we don't recognize all the zeros that surround us & we keep on investing, adding value, and multiplying in it. Then either the sum remains the same or we become the zero.

Even educated and experienced individuals sometimes face big falls in their personal or professional lives. When we try to identify the reason of this fall, we realize that it is because we failed to recognize the presence of a "Zero personality" in our lives, someone who adds absolutely no value and ends up diminishing ours. We find ourselves standing in the same position years later or even lower if we fall into the trap of such "zero" personalities. So, it is essential that we identify these "Zero" personalities around us and safeguard our lives from them if we want a healthy, wealthy, and safe life.

In the past, India has been ruled by Big Zeros because of which our progress was pushed back millions of years. However, India got back up and marched on to create its own value. It's we who can protect our families and contribute in making good a society. We must focus on our homes, and families, and try not to become someone's "zero" personality. We must not be the reason that a person or even we ourselves are unable to move forward in life. Therefore, we must act mindfully to continue on our path to a successful life.

In an advertisement we see that Akshay Kumar suggests investing in pads for the health of women rather than spending money on smoking which is not beneficial in any way. It stops the life of smokers from becoming Zero and promotes awareness and respect towards women. In the movie 'Udta Punjab' we have seen the burning away of 'Zero' lives. Cinemas are made on 'Zero' or 'Hero' personalities to make people aware of such behaviour and to educate them to avoid becoming zero. We all are wise & need to understand 'Zero' to avoid becoming Zero.

8.

MY BIRTHDAY-2DAY

I am pleased to inform you all that today is my Birthday. The day starts with lots of wishes, gifts and ends with giving parties to others. It is a day of pleasure for me and others too. We are born because of our mothers and she is re-born because of us. So how can it be our birthday alone? Our birthday is for both, ourselves and our mothers; it is she who has shown us this beautiful Earth. We cry the day we are born but our mothers are the happiest when they see our face.

Ganesh maps his life's growth every year on his birthday. He celebrates by planting trees, gifting essentials to orphans or needy people, donating to old age homes. We celebrate & remember few important birth events of that of King Shivaji - 19th Feb, Mahatma Gandhi - 2 Oct, etc. Many try to celebrate these personalities by adapting their values of simple living, truth, non-violence, courage, bravery in their daily life. If we try, we too can make our lives simple, and be courageous. Let us celebrate our birthdays each day by doing good deeds for humans and nature. Good deeds come back to us in due time; planting trees gives us beautiful flowers and fruits, we then share these with others who in turn share it with people they know. This way, we send out good in the world and make it a happy place to live. By law of nature, we are born, so let's try to give birth to nature as well. Sow seeds of, good thoughts, values and in return everyone, including us will benefit from it in the future. Birthdays are not just counting of years, it is used to correct, control ourselves each year to grow better in future.

Negative side of birthday celebrations can be seen all around us - lots of hoardings, noisy parties, crackers at midnight or during the day, or sometimes loud processions throughout the week, causing public nuisance with blaring loud music. It seems like these people have never or will never celebrate a birthday ever again. There is no point in blaring your horns to tell people who don't know you or don't care about you that you're celebrating.

As we say, **"A child makes a mother,"** so, on our birthdays and on all other days we should thank and revere our mothers and Mother Nature for giving us birth and for enriching our lives with beauty, love, peace, & safety.

9.

SAVE YOURSELF FROM THE WORLD'S DUMPING!

"Indore is number 1!!" – India's cleanest city award 2017 went to Indore. This achievement was not the result of just a day's work; it was the hard work of all the citizens of Indore along with the local government bodies, the bureaucrats, the labour staff, and use of updated technology and machines, that made the city clean. Songs were made on garbage collection and segregation to spread awareness, and timings were fixed for every locality for collection of garbage.

People aren't comfortable cleaning up their own filth but expect others to clean it up for them and for their surroundings to always be clean. Everyone marvels at temples like Akshardham, Amarnath, Madurai, beautiful churches, good

& clean hotels, airports, historical places, only because of its neatness & cleanliness. We visit these clean places but forget to maintain such values of cleanliness in our daily lives. We even exclaim in surprise if we find a place clean as opposed to the daily filth that we see around us. The reason why everybody loves children is because they are innocent beings with clean, unadulterated thoughts, which is reflected on their glowing, serene faces; whereas when we look at ours, all we see is stress, lines, and the result of a hard, impure, negative thoughts.

Newspapers are read daily in the mornings with people taking pleasure while sipping on a cup of tea and sifting through the freshly printed pages, however, the same becomes less valued in afternoons & becomes scrap in the evening. This fast life is resulting in a fast devaluation of many things including that of ourselves & other human beings. Nothing in the world is made for scrap. Also, someone has said that the greatest scrap on earth is our unused brain. So, we must start using our brains more for the betterment of society and also try using our gadgets and vehicles in a way that increases it longevity and decreases our dependence on them. It will be value for our own money, and will not allow its quick devaluation. Let us try and not buy unwanted things as it becomes garbage or scrap or space killer.

We are all lazy & selfish as we barely think of disposing waste properly and maintaining a low waste life. In the early days, we hardly ever generated so much waste and reused a lot of things. We stored oil in various cans & jars, milk in milk pots, collected drinking water from any available water body. Now-a-days, we can see plastic as a major part of generated waste & the most difficult to recycle. Let us try and avoid usage of any kind of plastic - containers, bags, bottles - wherever possible.

Like how hospital & industrial hazardous waste is measured & disposed off on cost basis by government authorities, similarly, the government should think of collection of garbage from homes on cost basis too. Should any home exceed the weight of garbage generated, then such homes should be charged extra for disposal of waste. Similarly, those whose waste generation is minimal, they should be given some kind of incentive to carry on with their set example. Let us come together to clean ourselves from mind, home, office, city, and nation.

As we have a hugely populated country, we must take care to avoid generation of Garbage itself; i.e. Kill the concern before its birth! All major cities & its citizen are getting badly affected due to the garbage problem. Pune, Mumbai are one of the worst examples of the same. Most parts of Thane are built or situated near garbage dumping grounds & are at risk. Many garbage ground surroundings are affecting the health of residents of nearby societies. Mumbai was built by reclaiming the sea, think of the weak buildings & the fickle lives of human beings staying there. We are choking our rivers and seas by making it a dumping yard, and nature should not be challenged this way, we all know and have seen nature's wrath. We must support nature so that nature supports us.

Working on garbage generation and management is a tough job & needs everyone's contribution and motivation, which seems to be a feat achieved by Indore and its citizens enabling them to reach to the top of the cleanest cities.

Let us begin a social movement and pledge to control & Avoid generation of Garbage!

10.

WORK & LIFE

Jagjit came home in a very happy mood due to his recent promotion. Others did not receive the same post. He became Sr. GM. Top Management was completely new, had new members & they want to make lots of changes. It was not new in the MNC culture to hire & fire for the organization, but it impacted many employees in Jagjit's company. His happiness turned to utter sadness as he was the culprit of significant manpower reduction. He himself was feeling depressed because of work pressure. He was familiar with the Indian work culture and the culture abroad as well due to his business trips. Due to his exposure, he uncovered important gaps arising due to excess manpower in his Indian company.

Unemployment is never a big focus point of governments. The ratio of vacancies to applicants is very high in India owing to its huge population. We have a pool of unutilized potential, and year by year it keeps on growing due to the mass churning of graduates and post graduates. But where are the jobs? Are we creating new opportunities & skills in the young blood through education? Demand VS supplies graph is inverted. Quantity of supplied manpower is increasing but there is a reduced demand for it due to automated machines, economic slowdown, etc. The real value of humans is being lost, Human Capital is being diminished. Here is the real turning point of life. Let's think again, for our future & our requirement in Life. Humans and not a big profit margin are the most important part of nature.

Our nation has lots of hidden talents, we must recognize those and encourage people to build and venture out own their own, which in turn will inspire others to do the same, it might even end up creating jobs and providing skills to those who need it, like the NGOs who support and impart skill trainings to the underprivileged. Let us come together on the path of improvement of self, family & nation. A perfect Square of equal sides of education, work, nature, & family is best suited for a balanced and enriched life.

Climbers exist till its Tree exists. So one must think about what one would like - to catch finger of a support like a child does with his father only till the time he is able to walk or to walk with his support forever becoming a burden. One should know & prefer a Quality independent life for oneself else it will just sink under the burden. A lioness gives birth to 3-4 cubs and goes approximately 20-30 meters away & sits there waiting for her new born cubs to open their eyes and walk up to her for her milk by smelling their way to her. Sense of smell of the cubs should be strong for them to live their life on their own, to search for food, and to survive in the wild. Cubs that are unable to do that are eaten by the lioness herself as they are not capable of living the Jungle life. So we must always strengthen our skills and capabilities for the betterment of our work, Human beings, & Nature.

11

CHARACTER OR ACTOR

We wear as many faces as we can. It's exactly like an actor's. But what is real is Character. Actors make action and drama sequences to create a role model character. Every person carries his own unique ways of life and chooses the best suitable means of living his life.

Character is always real & eternal.

We pay the highest attention to actors who are not real in life. We copy false acts of an actor & forget our own real character. We pay a lot to watch an actor whereas real Heroes

with iconic characters are ignored. We see at many openings, gatherings famous actors are called as crowd pullers, but rarely have we seen a man of real action being called.
Characters keep up the continuity of their devoted work for life & actor acts for a while giving a thousand retakes. Still he is the one to become a hero.

Now-a-days in the professional life, we are trying to adapt ourselves to situations by leaving aside our own wishes, ways, and personal time. We are in the race to the top not by our own choice. We are a free falling body. Where, when, or who we are becomes unknown to our character which we don't want it to be. When we realize what we truly want, time has been lost. We need to focus on our way of life, true to our character. After gaining millions & billions, one starts to showcase his clean character to the public. If character is so important, then we need to understand our needs to balance our life. Living a balanced regular life comes from being a routine character daily but everyone today wants to be extraordinary outstanding characters and want to become super iconic heroes of all times. To build and maintain a strong character, one needs to be ready to put in efforts, maintain health, and develop a learning attitude.

To understand someone's real character, one needs to study it very hard. A few minutes' interview doesn't clearly bring out a person's real character. Sometimes, a change in situation may change the character. Character is very important & close to everyone's actions and words.

12.

I 2 WE!

Akshay, age 8 or 9 was addressing the chess team on his success at the Srilanka tournament. He addressed the complete team and said "It was possible only with **your support,**" they were all happy to hear these words. Small, young kids understand the difference between "I" & "We". Had he said that the win was possible because of his hard work alone, the group's reaction would not have been good.

When we say "I" it creates poison in the heart of others or irritates the person. When we use the word "I" it shows that we think that others did nothing. Nature, parents, guides, and failures are some of the things that contribute to our accomplished feats.

"I" creates Ego & drives away. "I" cannot work with sportsmanship, in wins and losses, whereas "We" is a solid presence showing immense contribution, participation, interest, and team spirit. "I" remains alone & isolated, whereas "we" makes up a strong family.

Some senior leaders keep on saying "I" which hurts others because he is only capable of doing things due to his position & indirect support from others but not on his own merit. Once he loses, retires or changes his position, he wouldn't be able to do it as "I". Many people who use "I" are nowhere identified in society or at home. One cannot accomplish things single handedly without the support or contribution of others. One would not know Ram or Ramayan without the parts played by all of its characters – Kaikeyi, Laxman, Sita, Ravan, Bharat, and Hanuman. Ram Setu would not have been built if the entire "Vanar Sena" and even the smallest of animals had not helped. All of this was possible only with the co-operation and selfless contribution of people, animals, and nature – the "We's".

If political leaders start with "I" speeches and outlook, their votes and public support will start declining. When simple body parts start malfunctioning, we begin to realize the importance of each part. We don't pay attention to our hair until we start losing them. All body parts act as a team, always in synchronization and harmony. Failure of single part "I" is failure of complete body "We".

"I" is important in identifying the "We" formulating members, like **"I" as a rain droplet** to **"We" as an Ocean**. Without "I", "We" is impossible and without "You" and "I" both, "We" is impossible.

A musical instrument is played by individuals, but melodious songs are created and symphonized with "We" as a harmonized team. Doctors make operations successful as a result of teamwork & not alone. Every "I" is important for attaining success in every "We" event. Journey of an "I" is difficult in society without "you" to make life successful as "we". "I" withers away after death but "we" keep it alive in memories.

If anyone wants success they should avoid "I" and start saying "We". We should consider the world as one big family. If one has good things they should distribute it amongst others for their betterment, it will increase like atomic chain reaction I2We.

"I" may be powerful but "WE" is a Super power!

13.

NEED ANY HELP?

A young blind player of age 7 played chess happily. His mother, holding his hand, brought him to the chess tournament. We kept watching both mother & son and their happiness & sportsmanship in life. They have happily accepted the challenges of their lives.

I read a story about a car owner. Once while cleaning his car, a poor chap sitting on the side of the road was watching him. He came over to the car owner and they started talking. After a while of talking, the car owner asked him, **"Need any help?"** Even though the poor man was in ragged, torn clothes, he replied "Everyone requires help."

A rich family had an only one son, who had high

expectations from his family even though he didn't study properly; it made him lazy. He wouldn't work, or help out at home in any way but expected money for his bike's petrol, expected freshly pressed clothes every day, spent on drinking, and so on. One day he left this world, leaving his happy family lonely. We all need to understand who really needs help and who expects help unnecessarily. Here, we can observe that system has made a good capable person handicapped by supporting and giving into all his expectations and even with that help he was unable to operate by himself alone.

Some news inspires us by showcasing the remarkable struggle vs. achievement of few icons like Dr. APJ Abdul Kalam. Similarly, many scholars expect helping hands for their future education. Not all of them are of the same caste or economic backgrounds, some are 'BPL' – below poverty line. They need real support for their upliftment in life. Children whose families or guardians are no more due to any calamity or accident, need help. The Australian women's cricket captain was born in Pune & was adopted by an Australian couple at the right time. In all the above examples, we can see that the real needy are trying to break their cycle of struggle on their own without any expectations. They can be supported by governments, private organizations, individuals, or anyone who is looking to help and contribute towards giving such people a better life.

We all need to come together to make everyone strong & independent. Say it out loud, "We all are one."

Politicians will never touch the subject of **reservations** due to **vote bank.** Every caste is Open as a human being. Castes were made by man for identification of occupation and classes in olden times; like traders were Vaishyas, warriors were Kshatriyas, teachers were Brahmins. Now-a-days, professions are addressed by a common noun - drivers, bankers, doctors, writers, actors, and so on. The caste system can be abolished by humans alone, when they decide to come together and take a stand against it as one big community.

I was once teaching a class on Sedimentation & filtration to 4th std students and requested them to respond either in Marathi or in English if they understood the lesson. A boy, Imran stood up & said, "Sir I'm not Marathi, I'm Muslim." He misunderstood the difference between caste & language. The child's mind worked on the lines of religion and caste at such a young age just like how grown-ups behave in today's world, because till today no one has been able to tell the difference between any caste & humanity. Doctors don't treat any patient by caste VS treatment then why are our education system and governments divided on the basis of caste instead of being united by humanity.

When the army prays at 'sarva dharma sambhav' mandir, there are no differences of state, caste, age; just one goal – protecting the nation. Defence personnel are selected on the basis of merit & not on the basis of caste. Army ethics, their culture of unity needs to spread to every Indian citizen to maintain the Indian culture and to lead Humanity into a world full of light.

Everyone knows the result of demerit which is the downside of reservations. We need to improve India's ethics, culture, education, leadership potential, & work by promoting and giving a chance to merit based results and individuals & treat every human as an "Open" Indian category. India needs help from every Indian.

Life is such that everyone needs help of this or that, from him or her, for health or wealth, for gaining knowledge or completing work. We depend on our family, educational system, government, faith, & each other to get through life. Let us try and make the most of all the help that we get, like the child who happily takes his first steps in life making his parents the happiest the world. He feels happy because of the freedom he now has to reach every corner of the house without any help. **Why doesn't our government see the children trying to**

get up on their feet? Why are only some people being helped while others are left to fend for themselves? When are they going to get asked if they **Need Any Help?**

14.

WE - GOD'S GREAT PARTICLES

Look at children, their happy, innocent minds and actions. Look at nature's beautiful flowers; consider one rose, observe its enchanting make and breathe in its sweet fragrance. It makes everyone happy, and spreads a sense of serenity in life. Everyone loves to watch children and nature at play, in its raw form. No one is stopping anyone from being a person who spreads joy in the world and respects everyone. It increases the value of the person, when he brings joy to people around him.

We have created an unending wish list. We only wish to grow to the extent seen by our eyes. What we usually don't see is how much better we can be than where we are now and what we visualize for ourselves. If we incorporate consistency in life as our every-day behaviour, we reach our highest levels. We do a lot of work and when we pour our happiness, passion, and interest in it, it increases our effectiveness & efficiency. We can even save time for our family and for pursuing our hobbies. No one stops us from doing better things; the need is to develop a system which will aid in smooth operations.

We have seen good, devoted IAS officers, like G. R. Khairnar, Shrikar Pardeshi, Tukaram Munde, who, due to their passion and transparent work ethics have enabled an environment conducive to society's betterment. The career is rewarding in terms of true public service but they face a lot of flak at all times from public or politicians or sometimes both, for their decisions and policies. Good decisions, even though in favour of the public will not become a robust system if the public is not prepared to follow the guidelines or rules. People should use their power to generate a Good, Robust, and Transparent System for the betterment of society. It will not only reduce cases of bribery but will also kick-start the nation's growth. A good system can create the future of a child, nature, humanity, & Bharat as a nation.

Never did great saints create any castes; they were only followers of good thoughts of Humanity. Gautam Budhha, Guru Nanak ji, Bhagwan Mahavir, Sant Dnyneshwar, Swami Vivekanand spread their message and teachings of simple living, peace, humility, and love for development of humanity. Their teachings were so powerful, that even today people follow it and adopt their practices to live a better life as **God's Great Particles.**

If Anna Hazare as an individual can bring about a positive change in the system, then why can't we as a whole society of God's great particles work for the improvement of humanity, nature, and the nation?

15.

BRIBE

Government employees, private employees, politicians, educational institutes, police, doctors, sportspersons, lawyers, & many others have been affected by the deadly disease of "Bribes". Not a single area has been left unblemished & unaffected. Children saying, "I will study, if------" is also a form of bribe culture, seen at a young age.

2019 corruption index ranks India on 80th place, down from the 78th place in 2018. Bribe has made operations in India slow. Those who have accepted bribes can easily bribe anyone without hesitation, but that increases cost of living of a normal human being in India.

"How to curb and eradicate Bribes?" is the question

every common citizen in India is troubled with. Bribe is an attitude concern, arising from either urgent needs, blindly following others, or insatiable greed that no amount can satisfy. We should not promote this bribe culture now or in next generation, & this is possible by creating transparency, promoting humanity, and following the system's rules and guidelines with better control methods and corrective & preventive actions in place to curb such incidents. With the help of good education that focuses on overall development of a child, including their moral sense, we can hope to nurture a responsible and honest citizen of the country.

We are well aware that the government is now transferring funds & subsidies directly into the accounts of beneficiaries, removing the need for middlemen and thus, eradicating the leakage problem, saving thousands of crores. Bank account linked to Aadhar card has increased transparency & faith in good governance. Even though our government is rolling out policies like RTI and new technologies like e-tolls, e-taxes, e-ticketing, e- tendering, e-education, mobile communication, we still seem to be caught in the cycle of bribery to get our jobs done faster or for guaranteed on-time completion. India's ranking is down by 2 places, and now ranks on the 80th position in the 2019 corruption index. If we avoid paying bribes, then we can contribute in its elimination.

The day we are able to say that **India is running without agents**, that day every Indian will win and there will be hundred percent confidence and transparency in the functioning of the country!

16.

STORAGE ACT OF ANT

One day, Raghav showed me ants carrying a huge load on their backs. Then I told him that they can carry loads 5000 times their weight.

All ants work & stay together. They never allow objects to fall while walking or climbing due to fault of other ants. They follow their path. They are not seen fighting with each other, probably due to their excellent teamwork. They just keep on doing their work in a synchronized manner. They store their food & make their own community shelters called ant colonies. They don't overtake each other. They follow their path. There are no accidental casualties to any by an ant. They don't want to come first in any race of life. They share and store food for their community. Even though their total weight on earth is as much as all humans combined, they stay & preserve nature. Their growth is slow & unending! They don't take any loans to build their shelter. They don't go for health insurance. They work smoothly in the system.

We humans make a great mockery of humanity and of the lives that ants live. We stay together for selfish reasons and break human relations. We overrule the rules. We make the system to break the system. We are always in a race to win something or to remain on top. The machines and gadgets that we use have become like our body part, without which we can't seem to survive. Our communication is so "excellent" that it confuses people at every stage & keeps on changing at every turn. We don't utilize our energy to help each other. We stay together in society but lay claims like a ruler & behave like a King. We dig holes in our earth for mining and oil excavation only to kill ourselves and the entire nature in the process. We are behaving like Sheikh Chilli, cutting off support of our own lives.

We must respect the nature and other living beings, offer love to the world and strive to work and live in harmony, just like the ants!

17.

WHERE AM I?

Everyone is working hard to get better posts, position, rank etc. It's a race of life, we start running from wherever we are placed or dropped. We are born in one province or state of any country, and then we start running our show from thereon.

When we sit in cars, buses, trains, planes, there are differences in seating, so we find different views in different seats; same is the case with our positions & functions. When we sit on driver's seat we feel the difference between driver & passenger, when we sit as a passenger we feel the difference of other fellow travelers inside & outside both. It's our own mind which keeps on looking for differences. It's never satisfied & always looks at the greenery on the other side. We always feel that others are happier & the problem is with our own life only.

One day I asked my wife, "What is my company's name," immediately my son popped up and answered correctly. Next, I asked her if she knew what my rank was, no answer was received. I then asked a little difficult question, whether anyone knew my basic salary, she replied, "You are important for me, not how much you earn." What I do inside the organization is not known to many people, even those who are close to me & the same situation holds for me with others. I realized that organization, function, & rank are less important for people close to us, what is important is the individual himself. Still, we run for the human defined "Mrugjal" ranks. No rank will ever be a permanent identity. When you check with your personal relations, you will find that you are important to your close ones alone & nobody else. Your work, efforts, support, good thoughts, sportsmanship, skills, & many more points of your identity may be required by your family, society, & organizations but it is You & Your presence that is first important for your family. Still we feel greatness in our progress at our functional ranks. Think of it. The only thing making us unhappy is our own thinking. We must think better, brighter, & bigger!

We see that usually the skills, efforts that we put in, rarely match the rewards that we get. So we always plan our expenses and future considering the returns we usually get. We must know that we work as a multi-functional team to make a complete, functional product. One day, a manager asked his team to show their individuals skills; he asked them to go to the market & earn money by doing good business & not by begging, or theft, or by showing their ranks & organization. By the end of the day, everyone came with hardly hundred rupees in hand. The manager said, "This is your real valued amount as an individual. With more efforts, concentration, & time you can earn more. Here, in the organization since you learn & earn together as a good team, you grow together and are rewarded together."

So, to keep businesses and oneself growing, one must work as a team & not as an individual.

18.

LEADER OF RACING CHAIR!

Everyone wanted to be the Captain of the ship, so everyone was in the race. Some were running towards the ship, some jumped in the water to reach the ship, others tried to jump from air with parachute. Looking at all those who were running from all ends, one fisherman also jumped close to the ship when it was about to leave coast & went up aboard the ship along with the anchor. The existing captain praised him for his bravery and signaled for removal of anchor. The fisherman replied, "I did nothing." He was then served good food, and was showered with lavish gifts. The Captain answered, "I know you did nothing, but at least you did not chase for my replacement. The men you saw chasing for MY chair were sent to death. I need a brave person like you to drive my ship."

Politicians run the show for a while only. No one knows who the past CEO or COO of the organization was but everyone tries to reach the chair of the same by all means. Same is with trying to remember our great grandfather's or great great grandfather's name, work etc. - we won't know. Then after a while of us being gone, who will know us? Still we are in a race.

Once a Colonel of a battalion did not want to teach his subordinates out of fear that they are brilliant & will take over charge of his position. In a battle, his weak battalion became an entry point for enemies & then he got killed in the incident by the enemy. He put himself and his entire team in harm's way by this display of insecurity and weak character. Without proper vision one can't be a leader. In the name of good leadership, bad leaders are trying to showcase themselves as good leaders.   Many organizations are affected by Politics. It's not good for organizations & for employees too. It misleads the organizational ship, which hampers products, costs, the entire business, & the economy of the nation. Selfishness, eagerness, ego, lobbying is the form of poor political mentality. A Leader should have good ethics, command high respect, and have a great vision for the betterment of everyone i.e. organization, employees, market, nation, environment etc.

Nature's cycle, real growth is affected badly by the political self. Hoardings and banners are erected for no reason, and don't help anyone. Media is focusing in reverse direction of the reality of life. We must try to avoid race of life every day from everyone everywhere.

LOVE Environment & Humanity to LEAD the World!

19.

FEAR & FIGHT

I keep on listening to my wife, she tells me, "You speak a lot with outsiders & not with me." One who fears cannot fight, but more often than not one who fears also fights. Where there is fear, there is fight. Ants, snakes, dogs, cats bite due to fear. People who fight at home show aggression at home, but outside of their home behave politely & professionally and try to create a model image of themselves out of fear of getting disconnected from society. They can't expose themselves completely to external contacts, so they show their true colours to their family members whom they take for granted. This behaviour slowly changes the personality.

One does not need any subject for argument i.e. "No subject" in itself can be a starting point of argument. If you have a good subject for argument, it escalates. No one thinks of eliminating or avoiding argument. Save valuable time & energy for family & personal life, say "SORRY" for unwanted disputes and arguments rather than becoming aggressive. With aggression, we fuel our egos & not our goals in life. Fear & fight kill humanity & nature. Fear of mind makes us highly vulnerable without right resources for resolution, and fights demolish existence. We must keep our values intact with less aggravated speech and more positive work. If you don't speak a single word for a day, you will realize your power and the freshness of life - just try it out. Mentally powerful people don't fight. As we become mentally powerful, we become fearless.

If we continue fighting our growth will be thwarted, it will be difficult to face outside challenges. One can't be creative when the mind is busy engaging in arguments. We invest our important time, money, energy, mind & everything in these clashes. If we want to positively contribute to humanity & nature, we must create trust & confidence in each other & prove the same for entire life. For a short-term win we lose everything when we find ourselves in the midst of a lonely desert.

We are missing the real attack on poverty, fight against sickness, bribe, educational cost, unsafe road conditions. We have seen many people fighting for property, insecurity, irresponsibility, mistrust, quality of life, money, ego, etc. If we keep ourselves involved in such fights, there won't be any time or energy left to grow in a positive direction. Problems of the world will remain as is if we keep fighting in the wrong direction. We all need to be together to grow, we need to support each other to raise the level of life. We have to bring love, better communication, peace, humanity, at home, to battle for the nation. The power of togetherness is important, no matter who goes where! If we die for ourselves we remain unknown, but if we die for others it shows real power & courage.

We all can either choose to work for betterment or for separation from others, we need to decide!

20.

WHY EVERY DAY IS NEW!

Yesterday was "the" fast moving day - my birthday! I can't hold it in my hands - my ageing body and reducing years of life. I have completed so many years they have passed by in a fraction of seconds. Even though I see my own photos, I won't believe it is me. But it is a fact which I know I have witnessed myself. So whether good or bad, it is me.

A photo from my garden of a rose was captured in my mobile phone and few days later my daughter asked me why that rose did not look fresh like in the photo. I told her that the photo is nice, but could she smell the rose? There seems to be very little difference in Human & machine life, but it is things like the smell of a flower, the feeling of a cool shade, and the feel of a fresh morning that differentiate a human life and the gift of a New Day from the everyday machine madness.

We invest considering the ROI which should be in multiples of original investment. If the ROI is more, the investment is successful, if it is less, it is considered unsuccessful; same is with our individual identities. Right man always doesn't remain right in his day to day decisions. Daily working life of teachers, doctors, politicians is not the same, even if they follow the same day to day routine.

Change seems strange to us because we tend to forget that we grow under the external and internal forces of life and nature and that we aren't machines that don't age. Humans have been given a Big Gift of Patience, but we seem to have lost it. Our brain is faster than any other speed & memory, and we have made it further limitless. We must take a deep breath and learn to enjoy the changes of nature.

21.

LIKE & UNLIKE – UNSEEN PARTING LINE

I look at my palm & its back-side skin, they both are completely different in colour, hair growth etc. Then I saw where it merges with each other – the parting line – and I could not decipher its start and end exactly. I like the palm area better as it is fair in colour, without hair, and used for various functions whereas back side of palm is unused skin with dark colour, wrinkles, and hair which I don't like. It felt like the two sides of a coin – Chapa & Kata.

One day, I was sitting and talking to my friends, they were looking at fair & beautiful ladies. One said, I like her figure, her face etc. I asked him whether he would be comfortable if his father, brother, or any other family member spoke like this and had such thoughts. There was silence all around. Subject got changed. It's "Unlike". That means the things which you like are "unlike(able)" to you. It happens in case of any bad habits like smoking cigarettes, tobacco, drinking alcohol, etc. Doctors have said that these things are dangerous to health i.e. expected to be "unlike" by all, but they indulge in it regularly by choice as "like".

Our political leaders & government authorities have lost the faith of normal public since what they say is "like" for the public but the final result is "unlike". Public is being looted for gaining pennies. Normal public doesn't have any realistic expectations from Police governance due to lack of transparency & biased work. VIP status image of rich people has diverted the public from the right path. Failure of education system is due to the setbacks arising from substandard teaching, non-transparency in work, available benefits, and the end result.

I don't like it when others jump the signal, but I like to jump it myself to save time – this is called expectations from others. True result is measured by taking into account everyone's contribution & "likes".

Like & Unlike creates our identity in the society. We should be firm on our good "Likes" for a safe, long, and healthy life as a good Identity.

22.

KEYLOCK

My layman's mind wouldn't understand the meaning when my mother would say, "Open your eyes & see the world!" In many cases, words have direct meaning but sometimes we have to read between the lines. At that time, I used to laugh at this sentence & show her my big open eyes. Slowly, with time I realized that what we see and what the reality actually is are two very different things. We don't simply rely on anything & doubt every stage & step. I have locked up my mind, thoughts, work, and everything else possible. I don't allow my thoughts to flow out or allow others to enter, just to have control over it. I have controls & borders everywhere like land, parking, home walls, Lock & key for Gold, office desk, laptop, mobile, childhood, youthfulness, happiness, etc. What is open now??

Even though there are locks & Keys everywhere we don't feel free & safe. Because of today's media & marketing strategies, we don't have confidence on educational institutes, relatives, banks, food, police, politicians, hospitals, etc.

We should try to be self-confident and try instilling it in others. We don't need miracles we just need to be normal, good human beings with no eagerness to be superior & extraordinary than others. Can we love nature, every human & respect their cultures? Nature is first & last without any Lock & Key. It accepts our pain & brings us happiness. It accepts CO_2 & releases O_2. Someone created this system long before our birth. We need to respect that Great Divine power called God. We have just started learning via science how water got created, but someone made this chemistry for everyone to use. We use it & forget as it has No Lock & Key. God has made every living thing to make this nature full of love & creativity. We have put the growth of every living organism at risk because of Lock & Key of selfish nature.Let's think of what to Lock & What to Unlock: -

Lock to Mouth, Ego, Selfishness.

Open Humanity, Love, Happiness, childhood, youthfulness, Borders, water, education, medical treatment, trust, confidence, and mind.

There are few things, which need to be locked up for betterment of life & many things that need to be freed. Many things of life are beautiful, we forget to see it. So, open your eyes & see the beautiful world around us.

23.

IF YOU COPY ME, YOU ARE A GENIUS!

"If you copy me, you are a genius!"

It's a real challenge of the book, to read, understand, copy, & obey the right things. Doing wrong doesn't need a system, but doing things right with quality & a controlled system, is very difficult. It's like you can copy voice of any human in mimicry but cannot copy his great thoughts at all times.

Technology can be copied to a certain extent but not the Quality. Quality is very difficult to copy unless it has a clearly defined standard, dimension throughout the chain. One sample cannot be quality consistent, but random sampling works as a certificate of required quality. Due to CNC &

computers, technology has helped a lot to achieve precise & defined quality. Doctors are doing many operations now-a-days successfully with machines & without causing much pain or errors.

Human is an indispensable part of quality standard. It is all defined by humans. Machines are working as per quality defined output. Still humans need to reduce errors to get consistent quality. Manpower and skills are being applied to develop a system where the goal is to reduce direct human interference in Quality output.

Focus on **First Time Right** quality. Do one job only once with all the focus and the right methods - it saves time, handling & suspected damages, etc. AI - Artificial Intelligence is the next invention to replace direct human engagement in terms of defined precise qualities in production. It will result in reduction of labour concerns, and costs. However, AI is a threat to the work force because you will find market value of humans will reduce, whereas those industrialists, who use modern techniques, will increase their own money power. Gap of poor & rich will increase. Human is a threat to Human & Humanity. Lack of quality work output made human himself replaceable by AI. We all work, but not everyone works for quality. Man made machines, and now machines rule man! Without machines, man cannot breathe. Man cannot think about a life without machines. We are machine dependent & not free. So, if machines hang or switch off Human & Quality also goes off!

<u>Quality comes from passion</u>. Many people are passionate about various things, so they are identified with the same. Different people have different passions, and to get high quality out of less passionate people or when there are cases of volume burden we take help of technology & defined measurable quality. It now cannot be differentiated from person to person & result of product remains the same.

Many companies are now looking at consistency & a

long successful business life through the motto **"<u>Employee First</u>, Customer second, & Stakeholders Third."** Employees are directly involved in product development & cultural process. They are the direct & first image of organization & also its first customers too. The quality of employee life directs the organization towards success. Human is an important part of organization & quality. Many organizations grow because of Human involvement & many companies shut down due to lack of human involvement like earlier textile mills, co-operative sugar mills, etc. Indian President's Best businessman award winner, Azim Premji of Wipro said in his speech that his business became successful due to company's employees who worked for customer first.

Human decision, vision are important qualities of any organization & work. Business runs with human confidence. So, if someone neglects human's quality involvement in the organization, human resource department plays a vital role in every organization to get employees to work effectively & efficiently and get the best qualities out of every human. Organizations provide many value added trainings to maintain human quality consistency and to inspire innovation & motivation in them. Not only organizations, but every home, every leader, & political life has either benefited or faced losses due to human quality. So, we need to create policies for Human quality development.

<u>Quality & Cost</u> are correlated - we can get high quality product at high cost but it is not necessary that every high cost product is of high quality. So, focus on better quality with optimum cost like. Controlling cost for quality is important, when it increases, ROI becomes difficult.

<u>Quality communication</u> is important for effectiveness in a time bound delivery, respect and trust in business relationships. Transparent communication is the key to success. It reduces meetings & increases effectiveness & confidence in teams.

<u>Quality is the baby</u> of Top management. It runs from Top to bottom & never from bottom to top. Putting Quality first is good for the product, the organization, & the customer too. Engineering is the mother of Quality; defined processes & systems make it easy to deliver a quality product. Quality has put its important values even in Code of conduct. Quality & brand image are directly correlated to the product & organization. Like how we care a lot for babies initially for their better future, similarly we need to take care of initial quality for life long product cycle.

Better Process, Better People, Better Quality, Better Product, Better Organization!

24.

QUA(L & NT)ITY

Recall your childhood, how you used to enjoy the fruits from the neighbor's tree. It would be really tasty, wouldn't it? The neighbors would get angry at such mischievous children. But those days have gone now. We have grown up, the tree is no more. But we still remember the taste of that stolen Mango. Finding a good ripened fruit, plucking it, & eating it was a team job, the one everyone enjoyed most, despite its challenges. One child would hit the fruit with a stone, someone would stand at the bottom of the tree ready to catch it, and some would keep watch for the neighbor. Everybody would be so silent that a successful escape was almost always possible. Sometimes we'd be caught red handed, and then we'd put on the most innocent faces and apologize for our actions, promising to never repeat it again.

I have bought many fruits, but none of them ever tasted like the one we enjoyed as a team of special customer expectations. Why do good fruits always hang on the neighbor's tree?

This always happens in study, service, & business too. It is Quality & Timely response which makes the difference. Any organizations, schools, and businesses who love their functions & quality of work and life, are the ones who grow. Automatically, this makes their customers happy. Business grows, there are less concerns & more benefits. Those who cut short in cost at first, bear lower quality output.

Less Quantity results in High Quality as it has better controls. So, high-class automobile manufacturers give attention to cost reduction by building robust quality products which will stand the test of daily use instead of direct cost reduction of products. Working with the goal of delivering **High Quality** will result in **High Profits and an Unmatched Customer Satisfaction.**

One can have a plan of delivering high Quantity & Quality as well. However, it becomes difficult to maintain the same in the long run like in the electronics industry.

Quality is simple, innocent, it speaks for itself. Quality is the inherent consistent behavior & not a one-time achievement. So, Quality is you, me, & everyone else who is responsible for development of Quality.

25.

GANESHA WELCOME!

A Great Loving God- Ganesha is welcomed in India every year. Ganesha appears in different images & everyone loves and prays to Ganesha. The God of Knowledge and Technology is welcomed into a pleasant atmosphere and revelry by the old and young alike. Ganesha is the power of new skills & learning and the face of biological, technical, glorious, & a pleasant, happy mind.

Green Ganesha is the initiative to clean society & solve environmental problems arising from polluted water bodies. People have taken up initiatives to only buy eco-Ganpati and make use of waste materials for the decoration, thus, taking a step towards minimizing the burden on the ecology.

One shouldn't blindly take Ganesha home or immerse him in the water at the end of the festival; they should take home the Purity of Ganesha's Thoughts. We should avoid immersing the idol in water bodies myths are not greater than the environment. Even Ganesha wouldn't want us to destroy the world. We need to be strong enough to keep alive our love & affection for Ganesha and this world till the end of life by being socially aware.

The start of any new venture begins by offering prayers to Lord Ganesha, not just in India but in Thailand too. There, the people pray to him before an auspicious beginning and pray to him every day for peace.

Let's come together for the peace of Humanity & for Improvement in Nature by reducing crowd for visarjan, thereby reducing noise & air pollution. Let's make this green thought a Big revolution of Big Bharat!

26.

GREEN IS RED - AN APPLE THOUGHT!

Day by day green is changing its colour; it is the change from God's gift to Human's Drift! Green human mind is now just a red face. God's human is the reason for the changing harsh seasons & endangered animal survival. We find humans everywhere in search of innovation. Man's innovation becomes a kingdom for him. He wants to change his surroundings "for the better", according to his wise wishes. No one is safe in the hands of Humans.

Trees are cut down and the animals that once occupied that land flee, and this land is then acquired by man. These trees, the animals, where will they go to establish their claimant rights? They are forced to leave their shelter, their lives, and their families too. No one understands their tears & cries of help. They keep on living with fear before they finally leave the world. We have police, rules & regulations, various courts to lay claim for human rights. What about animal rights? If any indigenous animals are extinct it is because of humans and the imbalance we created in nature. We are making holes in our own ship. We are trying to grab everything for ourselves - air, water, land, & so many other things.

Change is the law of nature, and no one escapes from natural calamities. Natural calamities are not just natural anymore, they are now the after-effects of human activities. As change is the law of nature, we all have boarded the same ship and we need to avoid making it bleed to maintain humanity. Killing doesn't give happiness to anyone, may it be trees, animals, or humans. So, protect humanity to protect nature. Abusive words, rash driving, tree cutting, hunting is part of the war being raged against peaceful existence. We must invest time in creativity which helps in building humanity & nature. Making humans dependent on machines has brought about laziness & has caused high dependency on mobile, car, TV, internet, etc. We are destroying natural resources & self by being ignorant and becoming machine addicts. All the land, water, air, tree, mountains, rivers, & every human and animal are resources of nature.

An apple green or red, has its own distinct value & taste. Every colour is unique and we choose one as per our liking. Meaning of every colour is different, so every person has his own choice of colour. Our favourite colour brings us pleasure. Colours exert a natural power on us which can be seen everywhere from sky to land, from flora to fauna. Flowers grow naturally & change their colour at every stage right from bud to the final flower; same is with the fruits. Humans change their colour when they get greedy & selfish. We need to allow our talent, thought, energy, to manifest for the better of the world, not for our selfish needs.

We observe many open things are unwanted like we throw garbage & scrap when we think it is out of use & time;

whereas hidden things have their own quality of values, which we avoid sharing. We change, the nation changes, the world is changing, nature itself is changing. We need to bear these changes either good or bad or change our self for a better tomorrow. We must be happy & enjoy the natural beauty always. See the nature's greenery with beautiful eyes of the green mind! With a green mind, we live in peace & everything becomes green like the traffic signal - Go Ahead and do better!

Green building, green revolution, water harvesting, wind or solar energy, battery operated vehicles are a good start towards protecting and improving environmental conditions. Still more minds need to think green to do green things. So, more participation is expected from all to convert into a green life. Organizational CSR programs are now supporting the green initiative.

Avoid burning of jungles and farm residue, collect the same to produce fodder, or material for building roads or paper. Many companies work as paperless offices. Small efforts lead to a big change & one must start at the earliest. Many people are becoming more and more aware and are joining the green crowd on the green corridor.

Let us Think Green! Act Green! Go Green!

Green Life! Green Journey!

27.

NATURE & I

I always like to click pictures of nature. Once, in the African jungles of Pilanesberg, I was trying to get photos of lions but I couldn't find any lion on my journey. However, I did come across deers, zebras, African bush elephants, wolves, giraffes, etc.

Photos of nature in all its forms give us great pleasure when we look back on it. Beauty of nature is not in cities & its buildings. Every day nature is different with different colours of the sky, land, bushes. A Lion is a lion at any angle, when he wakes up or at any pose, same with any other bird or animal. They behave naturally, without any fake identity like human beings. Young ones of animals or humans are the most innocent living beings on the planet and everyone loves taking pictures of smiling, playing, or sleeping young ones. Through these photos we see God's innocent creations and their simple beauty.

Most of the time, we don't like our own photos, probably because we put on different masks in our everyday life. We try several filters to make the photo look better but we are hardly ever satisfied. Different poses, backgrounds, make-up also sometimes fail to meet our requirement. Why? Because we put on an artificial smile for the shutters instead of being naturally happy. When we have a naturally happy and smiling face like that of young children, we too will take great photos of ourselves.

5th June is World Environment day, my earth's birthday. We must appreciate and protect nature not just for the beautiful photos it gives us but also for sustaining our lives every day. We are a part of nature & nature is a part of us, so all our photos and actions should be natural & beautiful. It should always make us feel pleasant.

Think & Act Naturally for Nature always!

28

INDIAN RUPEE'S RISE @ SELF-CONTROL

Indian population, dollar, fuel prices are rising day by day reducing the market value of Indian Rupee. This subject is very vast and difficult when it comes to elaborating on it. American Ex-president had said that Indian eating habits affect market & valuation of money. I couldn't digest this so I thought of contributing to increase the value of Indian rupee. I planned to control my eating habits.

I replaced my tea intake with spinach juice and controlled my junk food intake. Within a month, I ended up losing 6kg weight and I had started to feel more energetic than before. I did not crave my usual cups of tea at work and I felt more alert than ever. This proves that if one observes self-control then there is no requirement of gyms, and extra exercise, only control over mind & diet. Instead of doctors adding diet control in future, we should control it today to remain free from medicine tomorrow. Let us be strong and try to control our eating habits and maintain a healthy lifestyle, it may or may not improve the Indian rupee but it will definitely improve our health. Let's change ourselves before someone needs to prescribe controls to us.

When we gain weight, we reduce our health & wealth by investing expensive time & money in medicine, gym, & many more things for recovery. When we lose weight, we feel lighter to do many jobs & gain the gift of good health. **'Leaving something to gain many things'** is the simple rule of life. While spending money & eating, we are unaware of our actual needs. Our intake becomes more than what is needed in body weight or earnings, which makes life busy in Non-Value-Added things. Our spending habits have increased whereas control on required things has reduced.

Honorable PM Narendra Modi observes Navratra fasting for 9 days without food; it shows great control on self. We must take up issues concerning food wastage. When we eat only as much as required, there will be a lot less wastage of food, this food can then be directed towards those who are in need, like the homeless in the cities and those below the poverty line. Everyone should manage their intake only to live, not live to eat. This will aid in maintaining a healthy lifestyle and also help with a no wastage goal.

Let us look at what food consumption would look like in the next 40 years. Per person average food expenses per year is 60K INR, per family is approx. 3L. If we project for next 40 years of life, it will be 1.2CR expenses on food habits. Observing a controlled manner of eating will not only significantly reduce this cost but will also give us a healthy body. We can also help provide food to animals, birds, and people in our local area. Here we learn 2 things of control & giving up. We learn to give & grow – it may be respect, happiness, money, etc. With India's population at 1.3 billion, and food expenses per person at 60K/ YY, makes India's food requirement at ***78000 Billion INR/YY*** *whereas,* ***wastage of food is 30-50% of the same amount.***

Expenditure on food & waste management is a big challenge. Our foodgrain storage system needs drastic changes to keep up with the food production and supply within India. Cold storage, grain storage facilities with clean storage conditions and timely checks on quality of storage facility should be taken up to avoid vegetables, fruits, and grains from going bad or being affected by rodents or insects. Many countries depend on India for employment & food. We need to keep supporting them while also improving ourselves; we are stronger when we grow together.

Swachha Bharat Abhiyan is not only cleaning of our surroundings, home, hospitals etc. it is really the cleaning of mind, Soul, & body too. A clean home, clean body, clean soul make us feel lighter & also energizes us. We must also detox our emotions and eating habits.

Make space for Peace & make time for soul & body cleansing!

29.

H&W BALANCE SHEET!

Sometimes we don't value & respect good things in ourselves. We fail to realize the importance of our values, health, knowledge, time, family, friends, nation, and nature.

'We can't book profit without losses', is the first law of life's accounts. There is no balance sheet with profits alone in any venture. So, every business has a Profit & Loss balance sheet. If we keep looking to avoid losses, we can't be in profit. So, we must learn to invest & understand ourselves, our resources, & limitations. Proper corrective & preventive actions are equally important to avoid losses else lapsed time results in loss. Nokia kept waiting for a new product development considering losses study but time proved its value & Nokia's competition started leading the world in new launches.

Time has killed many businesses, its value, and its brand in totality.

Look at the losses, don't forget it & act to plug the gap, else losses will act like cancer for the product, organization, and people. When we are running profit driven ventures, we must invest in losses or budget losses for good & profitable business. No one can calculate or predict this loss. Our fear of running a successful business kills the profitable business. We must have the courage to openly & transparently face the gaps of losses with a positive spirit to make the business more profitable in the longer run.

Many a times we have seen large investments are made for high returns and profits. What happens when it is our own decision? When we look forward for a high & good ROI or profits, we either forget about the losses and ignore it, or we don't plan for these losses. We can't reach a destination of profit or loss as it is just a phase of life. One must try to understand the difference between actual profit & real time profit.

We ignore the factor of time in the profit of our business, even though it is complex like brand value calculation, we must have provision for calculating the value of Time. Time is never considered as an important factor in accounting books. We should take timely decisions as a deduced value of P&L. In consideration of only profit, we forget the main losses & and loss of time too. Every family, an individual life has a P&L balance sheet.

What is the definition of **profit – it is above expectation**. i.e. if planned / budgeted profit is 20 %, and actual profit is 19% then we calculate 1 % loss as per plan. We calculate loss or profit VS last year or quarter P&L. If we have acquired 21% profit means, 1% more profit than the budgeted plan. We always want to have a growing profit, which is not always possible. Why is only a certain percentage projected as profit? There is no limit to expectations still we consider market study & scenarios to arrive at this percentage and grab market opportunities. To retain end customers, many companies opt for low profit margins for a longer period i.e. ROI time increases with a consistent long business life.

Anyone may have huge profits, but he will still go & eat *chapaati, bhakari, & curry* from *Chullha's* at a prime cost. Basic needs of life have remained the same since the beginning of humanity. So, if we consider & control our life's basic needs we can increase our profits and ROIs of life along with happiness as a bonus. We must focus for health & wealth balance like work & life balance. Before we calculate Profit & loss, we must have in hand the calculation of **Health & Wealth balance sheet** for happiness of life which is the need of tomorrow.

30.

FAMILY OK @ 40=60 AGE

My daughter is 6 years old. She keeps telling me to remove white hair from my moustache & beard so that I remain young forever. It's what she wishes for her father and what I wish for mine. There's nothing wrong with wanting to be young forever.

We quote many reasons like financial stability, educational growth, enjoyment, job profile, etc. for delaying important decisions in life. But we need to make life better, as growth of life in terms of age & ageing is unstoppable. If we work hard for promotion in service, why don't we think of right time promotions in our personal life as well, instead of being too late or making life complicated because of various reasons. Getting hungry & getting food at the right time is very important, and disturbances in the body clock lead to complications.

Today, we all make use of massages, beauty parlours, hair clinics, therapy, chemicals, artificial & cosmetic surgeries. We need to understand nature & natural as well to keep us naturally, mentally, & physically fit. *Brahmavidya,* a realistic scientific method on breathing can keep us young to the extent that we practice it. We should keep away from addictions like tobacco, smoking, alcohol, drugs, etc.

Alongwith looking and feeling healthy due to pranayama, yoga, and running, there is also a glow on the face that will make us look young. Self-motivation for doing good things is really important to keep up the efforts & continuity of a healthy life.

If we all stay together like a big single family it will be a pleasure for us and will keep us powerful, enabling us to take good decisions and maintain distributed responsibilities within the team. We can make use of life's youngest hours if we're away from mobile, TV etc. Still, as we learn from mistakes, we will give it up once we face the same. So, everyone should use their young life, young & important hours, to make **family, nature, & nation younger & stronger!**

31

1000 RS/LITRE

With the rise of a few rupees in the cost of fuel, many shifted to carpooling. The reason may be anything like taxes, per gallon rate, government price control etc., and the fact is that one day the cost of fuel will reach 1000Rs a litre. We should be prepared for that.

In 1983, I used to pay flour mill 5 paisa per KG & now after 35 years in 2018 we pay 500Paise per KG i.e. 100 times. Earlier, Bullets, Yamaha, Rajdoot, Yezdi, Vespa scooter used to be the pride bikes for high-class families but now, they have become a common starting point for a lot of people.

Science is changing its phase from liquid fuel to gas to electric to hydrogen etc. Cost of every moving step is increasing, with every phase of science. Increasing costs, unaffordable prices of fuel is making everyday life miserable. The struggle of poor is endless, middle class is forever in the middle, and the rich are always in control. We need to change our living pattern in terms of consumption of fuel at home and for our wheels. Solar is the best source to improve life & achieve zero pollution. Also, we need to control our unnecessary need for wheels. Of course, increased costs automatically make a person wiser than before & much more controlled; it's like having a foot on life's brakes.

We can walk and use bicycles for sustainable living. It is very much possible that solar energy will be used for long distance travel as well. Reduced speed of life will make us think less but focus better on everything else. It will reduce excess or unwanted stress of individuals. It will give us a chance to see nature and experience it. Just take a look at the power of our hands and legs to feel the freedom of zero cost. Instead of looking at the costs of life, we must look at the gifts of life. We are already enriched with sufficient things to live an incredible life. One should match the natural lifestyle by maintaining themselves with the help of Yoga, Pranayam, and other zero cost exercises.

Life with mobiles and increased connectivity has created an atmosphere of fear & doubt. We want to be in touch with our close ones at any given moment. This facility helps us by keeping us aware at any instant whenever there is an emergency, but it simultaneously creates worries as well. Instances of "no connectivity" and being out of range creates fear. Science has made life easy but excess of this science is creating fear. We need to separate our happiness & body from increased unwanted science which comes at additional & unwanted costs.

32.

OPEN INDIA, OPEN PEOPLE, OPEN SCHOOL!

One day when Ganya went to school, he found the school to be shut. He asked the watchman why the school was shut and the watchman informed him that the buses were on strike that day, the teachers will be on strike the next day, and the parents will be on strike after that. All for their various reasons of syllabus, fees, security, etc. Ganya sat outside his school wondering why people get an education. Was it for getting employment in future or for doing business? Ganya, instead of playing or enjoying that day started calculating the functional days of school VS payment to school VS ROI of life. The things that have been invested in school life are valuable time, non-refundable money, and educational qualities which in return pay an unknown outcome in the future. On that day Ganya decided to grab what he wants to grab from school for his future.

What is taught in school is not what is required by the market in future or at present. Doctors & engineers today are very behind in getting back their investment in education. Imbalance in education system has created imbalance in the entire life, including the nation.

Activists working for cast, community, attacks, separations, reservations, result in schools being shut and children losing out on their studies. Mobs roam around on the roads due to provoking, suffering, or just to burn everything to create disturbances. Mahatma Gandhi or King Shivaji never did or suggested doing this. We all need to come together to make India a smooth functioning country for the betterment of every single human being. Instead of damaging public or private properties if we all come together we can do miracles. Every now & then without any prior information, people come out on roads to protest. Is it really helping the agenda or is it done to market ulterior motives, no one knows. Are there no designated forums to discuss & claim the rights or make and remake the policies? We have to work for a net result. We must keep India cool & open on all days.

We all belong to India / Bharat / Hindustan, and one should be identified as such & subsidies should be available to only below poverty line & not to any caste. Everyone should submit ITR to government other than the tribals who need real education & a safe cover to live a fruitful life. We all, who stay in India obey and respect everybody's culture. Few of our leaders have planted the weed of "reservation" within the masses, polluting our harmony. It's causing a chain reaction which keeps on polluting life & killing the masses. There is no net good result to either of the sides. Damage to government & public is damage to all of society; it also causes embarrassment on world platforms. Strikes, aggression, hard talks end in mild results, whereas everyone's efforts in the right direction make for a better outcome.

Even though government wants to adopt many of us, they are barely able to repay everyone. What could be the source of their revenue except Income tax & few other revenues like GST, licence fees, etc.? How many of us pay Income or other taxes to the government in the real sense? We all need the support of our government & the government needs support from all of us.

We also need to support entrepreneurs for better businesses and for generating more employment. It just can't work one way. Development of a business is a by-product of teamwork combined with great leadership, & is not an outcome of selfish reasons. Well educated people or good politicians should take initiatives to form and re-establish financially sick organizations on PPP (Public Private Partnership) basis. Finally, we all need to come together for a successful future of India. It's not just reservations, agitations, and strikes that can solve persistent problems; we need to understand the real need of employment for tomorrow. Producing visionary, kind leaders & a spirit of working in teams is the required need from education.

Capability, capacity, & caliber of every individual are different and should be admired for the same so that he is able to excel in his professional as well as his personal life. The skills of a doctor differ from that of a driver and both should be equally respected. Gandhiji preached the importance of "Dignity of labour" and that no work is beneath anyone or anything, we should keep that in mind and respect everybody from a farmer to a pilot.

Ganya kept walking silently, still unaware of when school will reopen for him to continue with his learning of real life, nature, & Humanity!

33.

99.99% - ADMISSION CLOSED!

Micron level score chasing. It's difficult to measure micron & there are high chances of measurement error too. Hats off to the new generation who participate in such micron level competition of life. We are proud of those who qualify and refuse to accommodate the ones who disqualify by single or partial marks. The people who lose out in this race should be equally respected but all they get are tears and dejection of not clearing the race.

There should be an alternative to accommodate such huge talent. We should not continue with this practice of inviting thousands of applicants for merely 10-15 seats. India has great hidden talent. We don't make enough space for this talent. We have created undue hypes around IITs, IIMs, IAS, doctors, etc. See the scores of 10th, 12th, JEE, NEET, either +ve or -ve or 100% marks etc. It's our own eyes who can see only shining stars. What about the balance? The world runs because of everyone's positive contribution. We only tend to give importance to those who come out up in the top. We must understand the great hidden values & talents of young India and put them to use. Every try is not unsuccessful so we should start investing our time, blood, money in making space for the talented people who can uplift the society and the world. We all must put creativity & passion into our work to create a strong self. We should figure out our own talent.

Japan doesn't allow only academic educational focus, but they also encourage learning individual subjects of interest. Our education is focused only on theory & not on reality or practical. Why do we learn? - Only for jobs. We need to change this kind of education system and bring in more practicality and usefulness with respect to a child's interests and his capabilities. This will help him on to his path of success and also enable him to contribute positively to the world, even if it is on the micron level.

34.

SELFISH FISH!

"Learn swimming from the fish!" It is best if we start learning from the fish directly. This sign board is put up in Thailand. Fish learn from nature & mother. Their speed of natural learning is very fast, right from their date of birth; same with all other animals and birds. Where are the "schools & classes" of these birds and animals? Man is the only such animal who has a high learning & development time in artificial schools & classes. All-natural living things learn from nature & live for nature unlike artificial learned human. For the sake of "Selfish" growth human has developed artificial learning centers. As human beings we are away from natural living life and happiness.

We are highly literate but forget the responsibilities of a human being in keeping nature safe. We disrespect road safety.

We must stop ourselves for a while to understand the **"value of ourselves"**. Our selfish learning labs are not good enough to create **"values of human"** it creates **"value of money"** & erases "value of mind". We forget to respect ourselves, others, and nature. We pay a lot for sight-seeing but forget the nature that is around us and close to us. Pollution and population has turned us into victims of our own crimes.

Our education is either making innovations like AI or providing valueless education. Education is also a bell curve in everyone's life. Generally, if we try to learn a lot, we invest a lot by creating imbalance in our life. We must start learning naturally & on our own from childhood as per our own likes. Learning centers today make us lists of **_"Do's & Don'ts"_**, but we blatantly disregard such lists.

IITs & IIMs can increase the value of businessmen, entrepreneurs, & innovators. It can also be used to help generate & establish good & ethical business centers, employment generation opportunities, etc. as per a person's interests and skills. They should have specialized learning centers, which can create effectiveness in the functioning of tasks.

The similarity between all amphibians, birds, and animals is "Race of life for Survival". Our want of power and our nature of "show-off" is killing every humankind in the name of caste war, power war, political war, etc. **"Learn to live"** is important than "learn to rule"; it will create a good human culture, enable peaceful happy living by avoiding daily unwanted races.

35.

EDUCATIONAL ENLIGHTENMENT & FEAR

"Where there is real education, fear does not exist & where there is fear, education cannot happen!"

Enlightenment is achieving the ultimate state of spiritual awareness & liberation. At the age of 30, Vardhaman Mahavir went to the jungles to live a life alone. He gained spiritual knowledge & attained enlightenment. People like him were the ones who were without "fear". They created value in their life which they opened for everyone to see and learn from. There are many saints who followed the same path in search of reality of life. Jainism, Budhhism, Hinduism, Sikhism were formed with the intention of humanity, love, & peace. Despite there being various languages, they were spread to the entire world, not for a piece of land, but for peace, love & humanity.

Leaving valuables creates value & makes one fearless, it creates light for enlightenment, makes one lighter & lighter to float from one place to another without obstacles. Their peace of mind was so powerful that it spread to the entire world. Books were written, sermons were given, and sculptures were made to spread the message of life to people.

Following the path of fearless gurus, becoming friends of the world, having no enemies, getting a good education, & attaining enlightenment should be the focus of self-learning & study till the end of life. Everyone needs to understand the importance of fearlessness and enlightenment in education.

King Shivaji tried to remove fear from the society so that they could feel safe and aim for a good life and education. His supporters worked fearlessly due to the confidence he showed in them, and also due to his supportive nature. Fear fears the young blood, practical education & knowledge, and devotion for the motherland. Fearless people have fought for the right to freedom, for peace, & for the love of the people. They have never shown eagerness to grab land, and money of others. They have never used the power of weapons, politics, and muscle on the weak & needy. It is said that even enemies trusted Chhatrapati Shivaji for his honesty, transparency, & safety of life, infact they used to feel unsafe with their own emperors. Confidence, safety, trust is not built in a day or earned with money, it grows gradually.

Our education system needs to be free from fear. Education has now become a money making tool. Marketing education as that of being of quality, confidence building, trustworthy, free of fear, enlightening, full of creativity, love, and peace is not enough; efforts should be made to live up to these marketed qualities.

Having control over speech, mind, and desires is the ultimate step of attaining enlightenment and having a peaceful, happy, and healthy life. Having a peacefully steady mind also inspires the people around you to aim for the same and strive for peace & harmony of humanity.

Swami Vivekananda has a strong following for his spiritual beliefs & thoughts. Good thoughts never vanish but multiply and spread far and wide. It doesn't create hierarchy, it creates value amongst its followers. We all are human beings from different lands, created to practice humanity, and spread peace & love.

Education is an art of developing children for humanity & nature. Time is a valuable thing and adopting right habits at the earliest and following them will only make it stronger with passing time. This is possible when we take responsibility of imparting quality conscious education to carve a better tomorrow for humanity & nature!

36

INDIAN EDUCATION NEEDS A HARD PUNCH

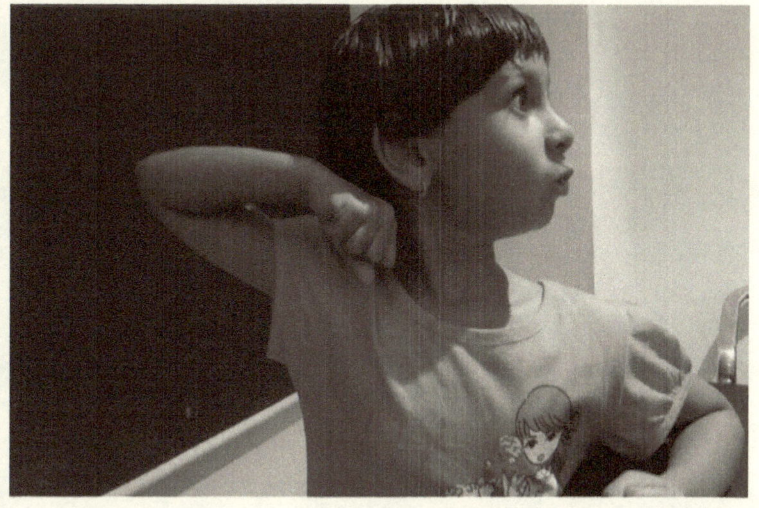

After hearing the cost of education VS future discussions, a lady turned back & said to me "Where & how will the poor's children go for education". Cost of education is increasing but there is no good realization of results.

Children's interest in education must grow and this can be done with the help of right teachers. Nowadays, teachers, educational institutes, etc. are available at cost & caste. It is the same almost everywhere in India. We won't find children of government officials or politicians going to government schools. This itself shows the prevalent quality of the education system. Even private schools which are heavy on the pockets have questionable education quality. A lot of teachers are not properly skilled to impart knowledge in an effective manner which hampers the learning of students.

A few movies like the Marathi movie "Umburtu" are showcasing passionate teachers who love teaching students and imparting knowledge. Some of our leaders have opened huge educational institutes and run it like a business. High fees are charged, quality of teachers is not guaranteed, and overall development of a child is compromised in the absence of good quality teaching. We exhaust all our energy in getting admission, paying fees, teaching our child post school, or further enrolling him in additional private classes. No balance remains for the parents by the end of the day.

Schools nowadays are mostly without playgrounds, in an unhealthy atmosphere, and having unhealthy food patterns.

Everybody has just one question, "Why can't we get admission in the nearby good schools?" Education has naturally been free but we all have turned it into a market place. Advertising has made it more complex & we are part of this business.

We all need to have confidence over the Education System & Educating Teachers for a bright future. Since we all pay education cess & indirect taxes, education should be subsidized, with zero cost facility of providing books, and conveyance. We have good brains, why not use it to make a good system. Why aren't all educational institutes under the control of the government having the same education pattern, the same cost everywhere in a diversely united India? We all need to unite for making education **"costless and of the best class"**.

E- is for Equal Costless Casteless Education for achieving a Vision beyond what the eyes see!

The future needs such kind of an education system as we need better humans & Indians with required skills & knowledge in all sectors like governance, teaching, medicine, science, etc. Savitribai Phule started the first school for women, bringing in equality in education. Our leaders must understand the need of every Indian for getting a quality education & employment. Many D.Ed., B.Ed., ITI, polytechnic, engineering, medical colleges have either shut down or are on the verge of closing. India & the world need quality manpower. We must try to match Demand VS Supply of market and manpower.

Below are a few suggestions related to improving certain aspects of the education system – *A Single Educational Umbrella!*

A. Admission should be given within a 3 KM radius of the residence to children of all castes, politicians, government officers, special needs children, etc.

B. Both private & government schools should be controlled by the Central Government with a uniform education everywhere within India.

C. All admissions should attract fees as a defined percentage of parent's ITR.

D. Schools should be equipped with playground facility & military/ NCC, safety & Yoga training.

Happy, Free, and Uniform Education to All!!!

37.

BIT - CONFUSED - BEAT!

A lot of efforts are going on in India to clean our rivers, air, and mind-set from garbage. Indore has shown drastic improvements with its consistent extraordinary cleanliness. India has become a dump yard of generated waste, with very little recycle percentage. From Clean India - Swachh Bharat Abhiyan, Narmada & Ganga Cleaning, GST, Demonetization, Military & agricultural development, science & space research, foreign diplomacy, bank mergers, transparency in work, VIP to normal culture, reduction in bribes etc., all efforts being put in are still in the development stage.

People keep paying tax on tax like Income tax, GST, education cess on top of private education cost. Roads are built for good but without establishing control on vehicle sales operations. Road accidents have increased drastically and have led to many lives being uprooted.

Private schools openly ask for advance intimation for TC, as they will fill new vacancy. Education has a business model now of high fees, private classes, and extreme unwanted competition which are diverting the real aim of education.

Value of excess money, power, and people is useless if it doesn't aim at increasing values as a human being and contribute to culture & the mind. One should understand that **<u>Money is the means to live but values and culture is life!</u>**

The public is constantly raising concerns against government policies and work as they are losing patience and are not happy with the pace of development or the state of affairs. The public does not want reputed names again & again in the limelight, but they need change for a better India & for the betterment of every Indian. People should **<u>reduce their talk & start working for India.</u>** Reduce the **<u>accidents & build safe roads</u>** with the help of proper engineering. We must **<u>focus & Invest in local businesses, people,</u>** & agriculture. **<u>Grow locally & serve locally</u>**. Storage of agricultural products, food, and waste products should be planned. Agriculture should be carried out in an organic manner. Local market with high returns & eliminating market agents will make the Indian farmer economically stronger & better.

Education **<u>should be free of cost</u>**. Every family's highest chunk of expense goes towards educating their children, but there is no guarantee of a quality return. The future of Indians needs to be safeguarded not only by parents, but also by the nation. We should be aware of our lacunae and try adopting good practices of other nations to make ours better.

38.

GREAT SPORTSMANSHIP!

It was a fun day for all the non-participants of the Rapid chess competition organized by the Gymkhana. The atmosphere was pleasant with light rains, there was greenery around, and different games were going on at a rapid intensity. People were enjoying the food of the club in the Gymkhana under the Banyan tree; it was a complete day out with the family.

Participants aged 4 to 75 were engrossed in their games all day. Each player had to play 8 matches. After each match, the children would meet their parents and discuss their game and the reasons for their win or loss. They would devise strategies for their next game as well. This is how life should be dealt with too, by accepting the truth & strategizing to change realities!

Why to cry when you lose, better make preparations for the next challenge with more confidence. Everyone accepts the truth of an individual's win or loss. In real life, we sometimes accept the growth, even if we don't deserve it.

Once a cab driver was talking about national leaders & bribes and how they have done nothing good for the nation. He also admitted to the fact that he was taking extra money and cheating his customers. He said that he tried long and hard to change himself and not cheat people but he couldn't do it. He had no response when someone asked him how he expected the national leaders to change the nation overnight when he wasn't able to change himself.

Without organizational support, one person alone cannot work for a long period and bring positive changes. So, we must respect and reward loyal work done for organizations & nations. This is sportsmanship - to accept the prevailing situation & work for a better change.

39.

A RICH PARK

"Poor are those who have more vehicles." Everyone laughed at this joke. But when you think about it, it made sense. Look at the cars taking 90 minutes to cover 6Km then look at the person walking on foot covering the same distance within 60 minutes.

We are introducing non-value-adding activities like driving, and polluting not only our own time but also the environment, mind, and health for a life time. When we don't invest in cars, there is no irritation, no tension, & no worries about the cost of idle running vehicles, its maintenance cost, depreciation cost, & mainly where to park. Many factors like police, signals, license, PUC, parking space, threat of vehicle stealing, and damages or scratches become a reason for our tension. Due to the growing traffic & shrinking parking space, India's Cabinet Minister wisely requested the public to not buy cars.

Ola, Uber & many other apps have made travelling at finger tips easy. It is safe, can be availed at any time, no maintenance or parking cost involved, and the mind is free from constant worries of theft or damage. **Put this saved money safe in banks and invest in other essential things.**

We used to travel in our own vehicles for maintaining status in the society, but the situation is not the same today as it has started to become a real devaluation of money & also of human lives:

1. <u>Playground need</u> - We used to play a lot in open spaces in our child hood, but where will our children play? They don't have sufficient space to play so they start playing on roads. Grounds are not available, either they are already occupied or paid. We should stop this unsafe playing on roads and make space by clearing parking spaces for them.

2. <u>Car & Parking devaluation</u> - If we buy a car, we need to buy a parking space for it too, which may be equivalent to or more than the cost of the car, or 10% of the value of your flat. Look at the devaluation and blockage of money. If you don't buy a parking space, the cost of your flat comes down considerably.

3. <u>Cost to Individual</u> - Suppose you buy a car worth 9Lakh INR and after a few years its reading is 3Lakh kms. So, it's per KM run cost is 3RS without considering interest (15L), depreciation (-2.5L), driver's salary (12L), washing (0.54L), maintenance (3L), fueling (6.3L), parking (6L) etc. So, total cost is 50L. Average cost of per KM run will go up to 9 Rs. per KM. With 50L in hand, you can buy a new big home without parking & with children's playground.

A wise builder had a promotional advertise that said affordable houses with, **"A Rich Park - for Children & not for Car"**

40.

FAST IS FURIOUS 9

Everyone likes races. Fast races are crazy and are depicted as a fun activity in the cinema. It's shown as a journey of Fast life ending Fast!

India is wasting its young blood on a fast track life. Accidents are increasing day by day, and there is no root cause analysis for the same; full proof action is also not taken. Young blood is very costly. A lot of our youth dies in accidents, militancy, due to illnesses, and on our borders, daily due to some small silly negligence or overrulings. We must improve our system & obey it as a team, if we do so, every family on the roads will be saved.

Safety starts with the start of life. Safety is in every breath of every living being. i.e. as long and deep as we breathe, we are safe and alive. When we breathe fast, it is an indication of uncertainty & unsafe conditions. We all need to create a safe atmosphere on roads.

Everybody's - including the government agencies' - approach needs to change from containment actions to preventive safe actions. We can & need to reduce the pressure of timely delivery, emergency condition drive, sleepy drives, visibility concerns, detection methods like year of pollution certificate, drink & drive, monitoring use of mobiles during driving, and overconfident drivers etc.

When on drives, we observe that many people don't care for themselves or the safety of others; we need to sensitize such people to the importance of living a safe life. We complain when something bad happens, but we need to start complaining before anything bad happens with anyone. Time, money, and life are more important than better plans. We must raise alarms to bring about good governance with everyone's collective efforts.

Some pledges that we can take and follow to maintain the safety of our lives and also that of others':

- Travel during day time from City to City. i.e. Prefer travelling between 7AM and 7PM.

- Goods transport from 7PM to 7AM only.

- Accident vehicles lying on road to be removed within 24 hours.

- Scrap, hazardous waste - carrying to be done only in special & completely covered vehicles.

- Two wheelers to be sold compulsorily with 2 helmets.

- Four wheelers should run @ seating occupancy and seat belt should be used by all. Every vehicle manufacturer should focus on road safety of their end user.

- Drive in a safe and controlled manner without speeding

and honking unnecessarily. Also avoid special high decibel horns and silencers.

- Avoid wearing grey, black, dark blue, brown, or any other dark colours at night, as it is a hurdle in driver visibility.

- Use of Pick up & drop points for companies & not a door pick up.

- Police stations should be free of vehicles that have been lying around for years. Recover demurrage from vehicle owners for delay in submission of documents.

- Valid vehicle permit / registration to work anywhere within India, like GST.

- Vehicle scrapping to be done by government authority after completion of its valid life with defined reimbursement to its owner & proper closure documentation.

- Avoid use of mobile phones while driving & also while walking on roads.

- Prefer using bicycles or opt to walk to nearby areas.

- Respect signal rules.

- Avoid driving on the wrong side just to save time and fuel but endangering public safety.

- Visibility of rear indicator lights & number plate needs to be enhanced & cross checked for its integrity.

- Speed trackers need to be automated and used on all express ways & highways to catch high speeding vehicles.

- Prohibit your children from driving any vehicle without a valid license. Also, educate students on safe driving practices and sensibility towards pedestrians and cyclists.

- Vehicle health should be checked every year, like pollution certificate, noise test, light focus test, rear lamp visibility test, cabin glass test, effective brake test, tyre life & air inflation test, etc.

- For any accident, proper analysis & immediate corrective and preventive action should be taken. We must make related agencies **accountable** for any mishap, and also make them a party in insurance amount of vehicles.

Save lives on roads because safety is the real happiness!

41.

ROAD SAFETY – GROUND CONDITIONS

Everyday terrible traffic is observed in parts where there is "development" underway. Construction activities of metro, bridges, buildings, roads, etc., is essential for connectivity and development however, there should be a display of planned work with target of start & end date for the convenience of common public. Facility like a center for information should be part of display for reporting inconveniences experienced by people using the roads or any facility around the construction.

Roads damaged by industries, contractors, or nature are not immediately fixed. We must take greater initiative in holding the contractors and related agencies accountable for not completing the work in time.

Extra manpower is required in areas of construction to ensure that no mishaps occur and for minimizing public inconvenience. But we still see an increasing crowd of people and vehicles suffocating our roads and cities.

Although changing pollution norms, fuel consumption norms, safety norms etc. are trying to push the Indian auto market towards adopting eco-friendly measures, damaged and congested roads increase the cost of running of vehicles and pose as an additional burden on the public and the environment as well. There is added pollution due to traffic jams and consumption of fuel needlessly while standing still in traffic; it also runs up the cost of refueling. People also lose out on their precious time when they are stuck in traffic for long. We Indians take up the issue of safety on roads very casually, but the fact is every family is badly affected due to pollution, traffic jams, and unsafe road and driving etiquettes. We all need to take social responsibility to make roads travel worthy.

India has access to good technology, but laziness, fraudulent behaviour, and corruption delay the time and cost of every person directly and indirectly involved in the activity of building and implementation. Delegates travel abroad to invite industries to India, show & exhibit to everyone our style of working, facilities & recovery modes that we offer, etc. Our government has shown great efforts in inviting foreign industries, but it needs to scale up on real-time ground support too. So that one can write **"You can fly safe with our work on Ground"**.

Auto Industry zones are surrounded by **huge long 60 -80 feet fleet carrier vehicles** everywhere. Logistics in India works on month ends. Vehicles wait outside company premises for days & weeks paying demurrages. Some automobile industries need to support safety measures by removing such vehicles from roads within a defined time period.

Industrial sheds are made with illegally mined murum sand from local areas & dirt is spread on roads damaging regular vehicle tyres, creating unsafe conditions for all. We must plug such actions and take steps towards ensuring safety of public and environment.

42.

LIVE ME ALONE!

In 2013 I met 55 year old Ian in South Africa. He was a man who lived for himself. He enjoyed his happy life - Live me alone!

We visited the African forest together and during our time together, I learnt a lot about this "happy" life of his. Ian was a highly knowledgeable and skillful person. The way he carefully drove in the African jungle portrayed his caring nature towards wildlife. But his happiness came from drinking beer. He even said that if the doctor tests his blood, they will find only beer in there, as he used to drink beer since his childhood. He loves beer, beer, beer & then the rest of the things like his family and friends.

At the age of 55, he easily looked atleast 10 years older than what he actually was and I feared that his "happy" drinking might become a drinking problem someday. This fear came true when in some months his emails to me, post our trip, stopped coming one day. I learnt that he had multiple organ failure. His love towards beer had finally impacted his daily life due to his deteriorated physical condition.

Initially, he was being covered by his company's insurance but that dried up and then his family had to arrange for huge amounts of fund for his medical bills by selling off their property. His love for beer was now impacting even the people around him. With medicines & precautions, doctors advised for discharge. He was now isolated in one room, and was allowed to drink his lovely beer to a certain extent. This "certain" amount was way less than what he usually drank, and the frustration from less drinking started pouring out on his family and friends. He was irritable, frustrated, and angry all the time. He complained about everything, and this behaviour was creating trouble for freedom of movement of the family.

2 months post his discharge, he got paralyzed. He became completely dependent on the family that even with his independence had gotten tired of him. Now this illness had become an additional burden financially since extra care & help were required for him. Ian's so called good friends barely visited him anymore. None of Ian's family members liked the presence of his friends as it impacted their family emotionally and financially.

Ian's company, family, friends tolerated his behavior till he was not sick. But now that he was bed-ridden, and had developed a temper, he was the cause of everyone's sadness and irritability. He was moved into his house's garage, where nurses treated and kept him in isolation, away from everyone else. Only his loving dog - Macchi would be by his side. He began regretting ever having beer in the first place. He wished he had never gotten addicted. His close friends, his awards, money, and family were not able to make him better. No one even intervened and made him stop when he used to be fine and was drinking like a fish.

"Drink to live & live to drink!" was the slogan of his life and he lived his last few days in regret, drinking himself to his death at the young age of 57. Everyone left him alone like a sinking boat and he got what he had always wanted - Live me alone!

43

MODERN HUMAN TOY

Someone gave us good toys - mobiles and TVs. We invest time, money, brain, body, etc. in these devices, something that we will never recover and something that doesn't benefit us much.

Earlier, when kids would cry, parents would give them toys to play with, now they give mobiles and tablets. Not only children, even adults have become addicted to using their smartphones all the time. It is such a hindrance that the government has prohibited use of mobiles while driving, while at petrol pumps, etc. Not using mobiles excessively should not come from prohibitions, it should be part of natural habit.

Earlier, everyone used their own memory to remember landline numbers of near and dear ones. As memory of mobiles increased, memory of human's started declining. Phones have made us so lazy & relaxed that invitations and correct addresses are sent directly with a link to the map. Great salute to the accuracy level of new innovative technology. Aeroplanes also land safely & accurately with the same. We need to keep our senses sharp otherwise when machines malfunction we will be left feeling disabled. Our machines can hang but let's not come to a point where humans start to hang because of a machine.

We have started forgetting our usual routes also now & keep our mobile handy for known addresses too. Nowadays, schools have started giving tablets in the hands of children and there will come a point in future when they will forget to write using hands. They will organize shows of the amazing man, who writes with his hand.

We are making machine adoptability extremely easy and it is making us lazy. We have almost stopped walking & everyone is on the edge of wheel technology. Our wild adoption of technology is also killing human interaction. All our family & friendly discussions are happening over phone & not upfront. Mobiles may make lives easier but we must maintain personal relationships outside of messaging and calling to live a fulfilling life and not be dead like machines when they are switched off.

People have now even started buying smart watches like fitbit and apple watch which basically serve the same function as a mobile. What is the point when a single mobile can serve all the purpose? We are trapped in a lifestyle that has us showing off and spending money all the time for no good reason. We have reduced manpower skills by replacing man and his skills with machine & upgraded technology. We want to be safe in the hands of machines so we are willing to replace humans with them. We may be making few human lives safe but many are becoming unskilled, semiskilled & are developing a bad "take it for granted" attitude. We need to promote high skilled manpower as opposed to the use of machines.

Many researches are on for developing weapons that kill humans amass; it is not a good use of technology as it is being developed for the destruction of humans. Technology should be used by humans and not the other way around. Over usage of mobile is killing humans; mobile usage while driving is making life unsafe, screen usage of TVs and mobiles is making eyes weak. So, we must use merits of machine & not make it into an addiction. Can we think of living without mobile? Can we think of leaving mobile?

44.

LOAN VS LONELINESS

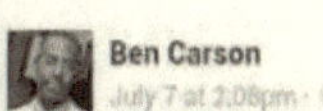

Try meeting anyone who has taken a loan and find out his real happiness. We can easily tell the difference between riches of wealth & riches of happiness. Cars are bought for fast travel & repayment makes life go by fast. House is bought on loans & we work outside this house 24/7 for repayment. Mobiles are bought on loans & getting an SMS of repayment on the same mobile becomes hurtful.

A state of mind without any burden, and with a sense of peaceful happiness is called 'loanlyness'. It may be an invented word but this word expresses the feeling when we complete loan payments & become free from EMIs. In that moment we feel proud, relaxed, and burden-free. Why should we not feel this way all the time? Everyone likes to have smiling faces around.

Loans help us get cars, homes, few other assets easily

before time but it won't help create income for an ordinary family. We keep paying installments that pinch our pockets and mind. We are burdened with stress & create wealth for financers. Managing loans is not easy & with the uncertainty that surrounds our lives, it is like balancing ourselves on a rope.

Loans taken out for education are however, necessary. Education uplifts the masses and benefits many people.

Requirement for loans began with the need for funds for education, health, farming, etc. Today, we have replaced **needs** with **wants**. Credit cards are plastic loan money that burdens us with stress. They lure us with easy installments and partial minimum due amount. Financers wait for the golden moment when we fail to manage our loan repayments or funds. It's a fish trap for life.

Loans are making us lonely. We must enrich our own worth, and live the real freeness of life. Instead of funding loan repayments, fund yourself first!

45.

THIRSTY WELL

When thirsty, dig a well! Surely, there will be many times when you will not get sufficient water even though a well is dug deep enough using all the resources.

We have closed our eyes to the excessive mining and overuse of naturally available resources like crude oil, minerals, water, etc. We are close to exhausting our resources. Water cycle is disturbed. Coal is disappearing, water in wells is drying up; it is an increasing threat to living things. The time has come when earth will take full control & regenerate itself.

A good system cannot be generated within seconds; it is more of a culture, so it will take time, learning, and awareness. We must make people aware of the prevailing realities before things get out of hand and something goes seriously wrong. We need to bring a control mechanism in place. Earlier, people would be kept in check by using the fear of god or devil, but now when the people are educated, they think they know best and refuse to listen easily or end up waiting till a mishap occurs.

We construct illegal structures, homes, grab land illegally, allow unlicensed hawkers to occupy spaces on the road, tolerate and become a part of illegal parking and excessive honking, and throw trash anywhere on the road, in the river without thinking twice. Even though laws exist against these activities, people are not at all discouraged from carrying on with it. Implementation of laws and fines should be stricter and devoid of bribes so that people begin to realize that no one is going to tolerate their illegal activities anymore. First few days, people will watch the strong action, then they will start learning & understanding the right way, and hopefully with time, the need for action and laws will cease to exist.

Better will grow & bitter will end!

46.

FREE OF CHARGE, FREE OF CONSCIENCE

Everyone aims to have a low cost life, i.e. reduced liabilities. Algeria is a country where education is free to all. Those who are getting education will also get free accommodation, cooking gas, & medical facility etc. It may be good for living a low cost life but it may create laziness in humans & cause an increased burden on the system.

In the past, taking things free of charge (FOC) used to be signs of poverty. Even a hungry person denies FOC things for keeping his self-respect intact. Time has changed man & now people take advantage of FOC without understanding their responsibilities. One cannot challenge authorities on how something is FOC & from where one will generate money to run this FOC show.

One who really needs help gets away & those who don't need it grab excess. All marketing stints are capturing this hungry state of mind - FOC, buy 1 get 1 free, free coupons of RS. 300, use code BD300, pass on Rs.50 discount, easy loan etc. One keeps asking for more without checking for real requirement because "Dil maange more." Jio offered FOC on their mobile service & now it is paid. How? When? Why? No one has asked them any questions. Capturing market is good but it should be ethical. It creates an atmosphere of bribes. It reduces the value of general humans & products as well.

Businesses are capturing & destroying good mindsets. FOC is becoming a vicious trend. MLAs or MPs get elected because they offered one dinner or lunch to normal public. Does it mean that they are elected for national work or for providing free food once in five years?

The FOC mindset has damaged the good people of our nation. Instead of building nation from humanity, we are encouraging humans to become beggars for FOC, loan, coupons etc. India is becoming poorer with this mindset. People become kings, businesses become billionaires in one night for a certain period, but it damages the nation & public forever. We keep chasing market, if he can offer, why can't you? We overlook quality and ethical service to choose the cheaper free one.

Credits, FOC, coupons, offers are becoming slow poison for Indians & human beings. Animals become pets when we start offering things, here it is us humans. Once human has lost his ethical mindset and conscience, he is slave to any market or leadership. People are kept illiterate in some towns to get offers from local leaders and remain beneath them as slaves for life. Now we even see educated people becoming slaves of various offers. One needs to learn & correct such behaviour, beginning from oneself to stop such working chains. If we create values in human, they create a good valued nation.

We need to respect human values by offering and opting for the best quality services. We have sold our own self-respect and conscience, forgotten our hobbies, real requirements, and have become valueless. If this continues, businesses, banks, humans, nation all will be at stake one fine day. Now it's time that we buy back humanity & correct the **biggest mistake trend and misleadings of the market**. Nations poverty won't be reduced, if we don't correct our poor mindset of getting things for free. Our **Nation needs to rebuild itself with values, culture, respect, use of national products, & not with offers.**

If anyone is Hungry, teach him to fish, don't offer him fish!

47.

TAX & WAIVER!

Our "Growth Budget" is utilized in waiver schemes for farmers, every single year. Income tax payers are investing their tax money in such **Great Deals of Waiver**. Master leaders of such great deals are proud of this event, the event that causes indirect losses to India.

Have any loan waivers made any farmer stronger? Farmers who have paid entire loan amount before, what is the benefit to them? Government needs to check the possibility of removal of dependability of farmers on evergreen loan waivers. Farm loan waiver addiction is not less harmful than any other kind of addiction. It is harmful to Indian economic growth. Some farmers are highly rich - they don't pay any income tax, their loans are waived, they avail all kinds of subsidies. India's "growth" plane will crash and burn on farm lands if the gap between yield, production, transport, and supply is not plugged.

If we ask all the MPs & MLAs & local leaders demanding farm loan waivers to pay their entire month's salary for farmers, will they do it? Never, as they run this circus show on the money of the common public. We, as India's tax payers are not getting any individual benefit of being an IT payer. People like us are many times thrown around like useless trash and rendered jobless due to market overturns. Where are we un-united citizens? Whereas, these pro-farmer leaders are evading taxes, holding acres of lands on their name, and have a political career spanning 50-55 years. How many farmer leaders have paid from their own amount for any poor farmers or villages? They just give highly influential speeches for their own individual benefits in politics at the cost of Indian government & the public.

Indian government should look into mechanisms that will wean farmers off the waiver fever and make them strong, like providing better quality seeds and real-time weather forecast and soil condition assessments to improve their yield and avoid crop destruction due to sudden weather changes.

Many articles and news are shown on farmer agitations and strikes but no one takes personal responsibility of supporting the farmers. Who is the government & who is governing? Do we not think ourselves to be a part of the government? Because whether we think so or not, we are a part of the government and the governing. Government cannot come everywhere so we must take the initiative for a good change and help the farmers. Every leader involved in the agitation should pay 10 lakhs, to show their great share towards farmers. Every broker must donate their one-day income to the farmers. Newspaper & media must donate their farmer related agitation revenue to the farmers. Don't just "thumbs up" like on WhatsApp, do something. The world will survive without money, but will perish without food.

48.

THE 4 HORMONES OF HUMAN HAPPINESS

There are four hormones which determine a human's happiness:

1. Endorphins

2. Dopamine

3. Serotonin

4. Oxytocin

To stay happy, we need all 4 hormones, so we need to understand them.

When we exercise or laugh, our body releases Endorphins. This hormone helps the body to cope with pain or exercising. We then continue exercising because these Endorphins make us happy.

Laughter is another good way of generating Endorphins. We need to spend 30 minutes exercising every day, read or watch funny stuff to get our day's dose of Endorphins.

Second hormone is Dopamine.

In our journey of life, we accomplish many little and big tasks, it releases various levels of Dopamine.

When we get appreciated for our work at the office or at home, we feel accomplished and good, that is because it releases Dopamine. So, appreciation & acknowledgement at home & work make every event successful and promote good bonding and team work. Once we join work, or buy a car, or a house, the latest gadgets, so forth, at every such instance, it releases Dopamine and we become happy.

Third hormone is Serotonin, which is released when we act in a way that benefits others. When we give back to others or to nature, or to the society, it releases Serotonin. Even providing useful information on the internet like writing information / blogs, answering people's questions on Quora or Facebook groups will generate Serotonin. That is because we will use our precious time to help other people via our answers or articles.

The final hormone oxytocin is released when we become close to other human beings. When we hug our friends or family Oxytocin is released. The "Jaadoo ki Jhappi" from Munnabhai MBBS does the work of releasing Oxytocin. Similarly, when we shake hands or put our arms around someone's shoulders, various amounts of Oxytocin is released.

So, with simple exercise, laughter, accomplishment of small aims or goals, being kind and nice to others, and by hugging our kids, friends, and families, we get all 4 hormones and are always happy. When we are happy, we can deal with our challenges and problems better.

A. Let's motivate our children to play out on the ground for the Endorphins

B. Let's appreciate them for their achievements no matter how big or small for the Dopamine

C. Promote the habit of sharing for the Serotonin

D. Hug your child for the Oxytocin

Make life happy with small things at zero cost!!!

49.

2030 INDIA INDEPENDENCE

India in 2030 - A peaceful land of humanity & world's largest economy.

Equality is not on papers but has been implemented uniformly throughout the country implemented with all its facilities available to the physically, mentally, & economically challenged. Improved transparency & literacy rate has finally removed bribe from the Indian system. Equal education is available to all at the cost of the government. Equal education has led to a significant rise in the number of entrepreneurs & businessmen. Equal tax is applicable to all on consumption of manufactured goods only. Revenue generation & taxation has become easy with GST. Every person's tax filing is done by government on every transaction & there is NO Income Tax!

Everyone is staying in government owned houses on 99 years of lease. It has eradicated unwanted and illegal house construction business & illegal sand mining allowing nature and rivers to breathe and flourish. Green cover is increasing, it is mandatory for every household to harvest rainwater and plant trees.

Government car pool, bus, train, sea, and air transport are extensively used instead of private vehicles. This has controlled traffic jams and pollution to a huge extent; the air quality is the best it has been in years. E-vehicles have taken over and charging points for vehicles have replaced the petrol pumps. We are the biggest consumers, manufacturers, and exporters of renewable energy in the world.

Lesser amount of crimes has reduced the pressure on police forces. Cases in courts no longer take a decade for resolution. Everyone is in a profession of their own choosing. There is no dearth of demand vs. supply and people are passionate about their job. The country is free of beggars and poverty.

Voting is planned based on E-voting and e-verifying techniques, eliminating the need to travel and to stand in long queues for casting votes. Election budget is redirected for funding research and development projects. Ineffective and inefficient elected members of any house & administrative officers are called back by public on majority vote basis.

HINDU (Healthy Independent Developed Union) is the religion of Bharat. Young, healthy, wealthy India is grabbing Olympics medals, and is playing in every international game.

Every Indian aims for higher growth in every industry, including agriculture, individual income. We all work together as a Responsible Team. Farmers are direct sellers, they are independent. We are working & supporting the world for the betterment of Humans, Humanity, & Nature!

Jai Hind! Jai Bharat!

EPILOGUE

Life is full of various chapters like articles in every corner of life. We need to clear every hurdle of life with ease to make our life successful, happy, healthy, and to strike a work-life balance in minimum available time, efforts, resources etc. This book showcases thoughts & feelings in every chapter which speaks about self-feeling & controls noticed & experienced in life.

If we want to recreate our happier childhood again, we need to be like children again for 360 days a year & in 360 degrees. Who is happy in life is a big question. To answer it, any individual can try simple & easy tricks, control their wishes, & fulfill their needs. After consistent efforts, we will be on the right track of a long, successful, and healthy life.

1st book published in Marathi language on **"Thought process"** 2016

When we change our thoughts, we see the same world with different eyes. Be positive always, it helps to reach our goals at the earliest!